Am I Beautiful... or What?!

**Outreach and ministry to people
with learning disabilities**

DAVID POTTER

Scripture Union

Scripture Union, 207–209 Queensway, Bletchley, MK2 2EB, England.

First published 1998

ISBN 1 85999 202 1

British Library Cataloguing-in-Publication Data
A catalogue record for this book is available from the British Library.

Cover design by Hurlock Design.
Illustrations by Helen Gale.

Printed and bound in Great Britain by Henry Ling Ltd, The Dorset Press, Dorchester DT1 1HD.

Acknowledgements

My wife, Madeleine, took the initiative in reaching out in ministry to people with learning disabilities. The work of Causeway PROSPECTS is based largely on her work, and all the teaching material in this book was written by her. I gladly acknowledge my debt to her wisdom and leadership in this.

The rate at which Causeway PROSPECTS continues to grow owes a great deal to the enthusiasm and commitment of Tony and Tua Phelps-Jones. I salute the energy with which they serve God for the enrichment of people with learning disabilities.

The title of the book is taken from one of the songs on *Beautiful … or What?!* This outstanding album was commissioned by PROSPECTS (when it was called 'A Cause for Concern'), and provides a series of musical 'snapshots' in the life of a young woman with a learning disability, and her family. (See the Resources section for information about our special offer.)

Some material in this book is based on or has appeared in *We're all Special to God* and the DIY Training Pack *The Local Church and Mental Handicap*, both published by Scripture Union.

*To all members of Causeway PROSPECTS groups
from whom I have learned more than I can say*

Contents

Beginning with you

This is me, the me you see,
    it's really all I've got.
I'd like someone to tell me,
    I'd like someone to tell me,
Am I beautiful, am I beautiful,
    am I beautiful ... or what?
From 'Beautiful ... or What?!'
by Adrian Snell and Phil Thomson (Nelson Word)

Imagine...

- No one, at any time in your life, had told you that you were loved, valued and beautiful.
- Your mother had never cooed over you as a baby, telling you that you were lovely.
- Never in your life had someone said, 'Well done.'
- Your attempts to express yourself were mostly misunderstood or disregarded.
- You had missed every goal your family had for you.

Would it be surprising if you were asking, 'Am I beautiful ... or what?'

Yet many people with learning disabilities will have gone through one or more of these experiences. It is still within the lifetime of many of them that a child discovered to have a learning disability would have been placed in a long-stay institution for the rest of his or her life. Only in the last twenty years have these places been closed and their residents moved into nearby communities.

This book is about ministry to the substantial group of people – one in 45 of the population – whom we once described as 'mentally handicapped' but now speak of as having learning disabilities. These men, women and children live in your city, your town, your village, your parish, perhaps in your street or block of flats. But it is possible that not one of them attends your church. Think of it – 1,200,000 people largely unreached and untouched by the good news of God's love.

So let's make a start, right where you are. For whatever reason, you have a copy of this book in your hands, and my aim is to keep you reading right to the last page. More than that, I want, if necessary, to influence the way you think and act in the future. Do you find this threatening? Relax! Once you begin to share God's interest in people with learning disabilities, you will find your life enriched way beyond your expectations.

Attitudes

In the last twenty years the number of people with learning disabilities living in the community has increased substantially, in spite of the ravages of abortion. There are two reasons for this: the first is general; the second is particular.

Like the rest of Western society, people with learning disabilities have benefited from huge improvements in medical science. Those who were more vulnerable to infection or childhood ailments can now be successfully treated and cured. The result is that many more survive into adulthood and old age, while the birth rate remains fairly constant.

The second reason for more people with learning disabilities living in the community is the progressive closure of the long-stay institutions that once housed them. By the mid-1990s, only 15,000 still lived in such places. What is more, the trend in the late 1980s and 1990s has been to house small groups in or near ordinary housing.

The strategy to move people into the community was called 'Care in the Community', but experience has shown that many communities do not care. In fact, the thought of someone with a learning disability moving into the house next door arouses feelings of deep discomfort. The general response of the public has been sufficiently hostile for one major parents' group to campaign for the institutions to be kept open or, failing that, for their sites to be used to create villages for people with learning disabilities.

Why the hostility? What is the perceived problem? In a word, misunderstanding, which breeds fear. All sorts of myths and fables surround learning disability: 'They are over-sexed', 'They are violent', 'They steal', 'They will escape at night', and so on. These sad, almost mediaeval generalisations still dog the path of those perceived by society as 'not normal'.

Experience shows that Christians are as likely to be afraid of people with learning disabilities as anyone else. This, combined with a failure to understand the nature of learning disability, has resulted in those affected having a very low level of participation in church life. It is not that they have been excluded, though this is not unknown. Rather, they have not been included, since positive action by the church may well be required if people with learning disabilities are to take part in church life.

Obstacles

You may protest that your church is as open to people with learning disabilities as to anybody else. In fact, this is probably not the case, for reasons that lie in the nature of learning disability rather than in any decision taken in a church meeting or in rules laid down by a denomination. A person with a learning disability may not actually realise that 'church' exists. She may never have heard the word 'church' or, having heard it, may not understand the reason for having churches. At best, it is likely that the word will only bring to mind a building she passes from time to time.

However, suppose someone with a learning disability decides to come to your morning service next Sunday. Could she get there unaided, presuming she knows what time services start? When she arrives, it is likely that someone will give her a book, or two. However, only one in three people with learning disabilities can read, let alone follow a hymn or a Bible reading at a predetermined speed. The service will probably major on abstract themes such as prayer, love, hope, faith, sin and salvation. All very real and precious, but people with learning disabilities have profound difficulty with concepts and abstract ideas. Their concentration span may last only minutes, making it hard for them to make sense of long prayers and sermons.

Do you begin to see the problems? If you add to these our varied church cultures, our standing and sitting and kneeling, then you will begin to see how bewildering it all becomes for people with limited intelligence. Yet they, no less than we, desperately need to know that God loves them and that Jesus died for their sins. If they cannot change their disability, perhaps we have to do something about our church!

Worrying? Many churches who have made a positive response have found their life and work greatly enriched.

Labels

One more preliminary – how to describe the people we are thinking about. Already the terms 'mental handicap' and 'learning disability' have been used, and to these we could add 'learning difficulty'. It is no longer politically correct to use the first term, though it is still the most widely recognised. The current phrase 'people with learning disabilities' puts the focus on the fact that these are people first, people who happen to have a disability.

That much is good. However, all the terms on offer focus on negative rather than positive qualities, what people can't do rather than what they can. So, while using the accepted terminology, the following caveats should be understood:

- People with learning disabilities are to be valued and respected for their own sake.
- People with learning disabilities are as valuable and significant as the rest of us.

Or to put it another way, people with learning disabilities are beautiful people, no less than others, with the potential to be more beautiful still through knowing the Lord Jesus. They need others to tell them both of their own value and of the divine love that reaches out to them. That's why this book begins with you!

Part I
ACCEPTING

Chapter I
Being human

At this point we may be in too much of a hurry. It is natural to want to find out more about learning disability. Surely if we knew more, we could be more accepting.

Maybe, but we need to take a step back and ask some more fundamental questions about what it is to be human. After all, we might take time to wonder why we accept those who don't have learning disabilities! What is it that makes us comfortable with some people but uncomfortable with others?

Tolerance

We are more ready to tolerate other human beings than we are to accept them.

Think about this for a moment. There are many groups of people we do not easily accept into our social circles, though we will tolerate the fact that they are there, somewhere not far away. It may become stressful for us if they get too close to where we are, enjoying our snug existence.

Take other people's children, for example. We are willing to accept our own, but the wildly out-of-control little delinquents from the notorious council estate down the road are a different matter – unless they are willing to conform to our standards, of course. We are pleased when the doorbell tells us we have visitor – until we discover that it's some smelly tramp asking for a glass of water, or a skinhead selling dusters. We may tolerate such people, but *accepting* them is something else.

None of this will be news to you! It is a fact of life that we tend to divide into different social, ethnic and age groups. Immigrants from the same country often cluster in the same district – think of Bradford, or Southall in London. Elderly people gravitate to bungalow developments near the coast, or retirement apartments elsewhere. Young families are frequently found on new housing estates. The fact that we do differentiate between different groups of people does not necessarily challenge what others are or what they do. So long as they don't demand our acceptance, we can tolerate their differentness. They are people like us, after all.

The key to the question

Which brings us to the heart of the issue: what is it that makes people people? What is a human being? Of all the questions Christians need to face today, this must be one of the most fundamental. If we are not clear on this point, we rob ourselves of a moral basis for society and community. We expose our babies to abortion and our elderly and disabled friends to euthanasia. We need some clarity here if we are to tackle questions about issues such as homelessness, unemployment, the quality of life, poverty, third-world debt, gender, famine – and many more.

I find it strange that you will not find many books on this vital subject in your local Christian bookshop. A thorough treatment would take more space than is available here, but if we can find an answer that expresses the essence of what the Bible says, we will discover what our response to people with learning disabilities ought to be. Whether or not we accept them, as distinct from tolerating them, depends on whether or not we believe that they are, in fact, people.

Before you respond that it is monstrous to suggest otherwise, let me ask this: have you ever behaved towards a person with a learning disability as though he didn't exist? In other words, have you never treated him as a non-person?

To decide what makes us human, we need to find some sort of measure, some simple definition or principle that will include everyone who is a human being and exclude everything that is not. It must work for every period of history, every social or tribal group, every creed, every colour and every race. This definition must be universally true, and it had better be easy to apply so that no one has to endure being treated as subhuman while a committee deliberates on their status!

No problem. The Bible answered that question long before we asked it. Genesis 1 sets the scene of time, history and all things with two crucial statements: the first (v1) tells us that God exists and who he is. The second (vs26–27) tells us who and what we are. These are foundation statements which enable us to understand life and meaning in a way we could never have discovered unaided. They tell us how and why we are so alike, while, at the same time, they assume that there are differences between us.

Let's unpack this. The Bible says that we are 'made in God's image and likeness' (vs26–27). What does this mean? Clearly it does not relate to our appearance – not least because God does not have a physical body – but, rather, to our moral, spiritual, intellectual and emotional faculties. If you consider the ways in which people are like God, as he has revealed himself in the Bible, you will begin to discern a number of characteristics. For example:

- We can exercise dominion or control over the created world (v28).
- We are social beings (1:26; 2:18) and have a capacity for forming deep personal relationships.
- We have consciences that help us distinguish what is right from what is wrong (3:22).
- We can think rationally, make decisions and reflect on what we have done.
- We can appreciate beauty and be creative.

And to these we could add that we have a sense of humour!

The degree to which any of these characteristics is found in a person does not make that person more or less human. We do not think of an artist as more human than an athlete, or a shy person as less human than a bumptious one. This determining principle from Genesis is universally true – it includes people of all sorts and sizes. At the same time, it excludes what is *not* human (animals that walk on two legs or birds that 'talk' cannot meet these criteria).What is more, this principle recognises all the faults, flaws and failings in human beings, but at the same time says to them, 'You are wonderful.' By becoming human in the person of Jesus, God has shown that to be human is not something to be ashamed of.

By now you can see how relevant this is to our theme. It shows that people with learning disabilities are to be counted as 'in' whenever we talk about human beings. They may have different levels of skill within those Godlike characteristics, but they share them with the rest of us. And if God's word allows for their inclusion as people, it follows that what God desires for people he desires for them. This is the first step towards our accepting them.

Some may protest that I am not being realistic. After all, people with learning disabilities *are* 'different'!

Of course they are – differentness is an essential part of being human. You see it right there in Genesis: 'So God created man in his own image, in the image of God he created him; male and female he created them' (1:27). Human beings were made male and female! Right from the start there were substantial and noticeable differences between them. It is almost as if God is drawing our attention to the diversity that exists among people. Even if we consider the men and women we know, we will find that there are substantial differences between members of the same sex.

All of which we know and expect. We would be flabbergasted to walk into church and find that every person in the congregation looked exactly like ourselves (nightmares are made of this!). Why then do we have such a problem with differentness? Maybe it is because we have established too narrow boundaries within which we will accept it. We may tolerate people outside those boundaries, but feel that they have to change before they can be among those we accept. However understandable this may be, however 'normal', it is an outlook the Bible challenges us to abandon!

Making the principle practical

To make allowance for our differentness, and to be accepting of one another, we need to set out what each of us ought to be able to expect in terms of rights, privileges, opportunities and responsibilities. Using the clues the Bible has given us, we can discover what it is that we value for ourselves and then see how we should extend this to people with learning disabilities. There are six elements we can build on to achieve this, and they are interlinked and mutually dependent. Together they form a principle which we could call the Principle of Personal Value.

1 INDIVIDUALITY

It is common for people to think of those who have a learning disability as a group who are more like each other than they are like other people. So, as we touched on earlier, you may hear it said, 'They all love music', 'They are loveable people' or 'They are violent'. To make generalisations which are expected to apply to 1.2 million different human beings is simply ludicrous. Like any group or category of people, those with learning disabilities are as diverse as they are numerous: one dresses smartly, another casually; one loves sport, another loathes it; one likes sunshine, another prefers rain – and so on. Every person – with or without a learning disability – is an individual.

We should expect and encourage that individuality. At least this should stop us talking of 'the mentally handicapped' or 'the learning disabled', as if they were all identical to one another. And it should mean that we set aside the myths we have heard about people with disabilities so that we can meet them as individuals in their own right.

2 INTEGRITY

We usually think of integrity in terms of personal honour, and this, in turn, comes from the choices we make. We expect to be trusted to make rational and sensible decisions. So we decide where we live and work, how we spend our leisure, what we spend our money on, and a myriad other things.

Such ordinary human experiences have been largely denied people with learning disabilities on the grounds that they are incapable of making such decisions or that they would make the wrong ones. As a result, they may have no say in even the small choices, like when to go to bed, let alone the big choices, like where or with whom they will live when they leave the parental home. Mike was over 75 before he was asked what colour he would like his room decorated! And imagine being told that from next week you were going to have to live in another house, that you would be saying goodbye to your friends, and not have any say in where or with whom you would spend the next years of your life.

Or the choices offered may be non-choices. Imagine being asked if you would like to wear the green tie or the orange one, when what you really wanted was not to wear a tie at all! Or whether you would like to go to Butlins in Bognor or Skegness for a holiday, when what you wanted was to go camping!

All these things have been part of the daily injustice suffered by people with learning disabilities at the hands of those who have failed to see that being able to choose means being able to choose with integrity. Perhaps their greatest enemies may be well-meaning friends, staff or relatives?

3 INDEPENDENCE

On the one hand, we all want it as we struggle through our teenage years, challenging our parents long-term control over our lives. Then we discover that independence is a chimera, that we are never really on our own. Our lives are inextricably linked to other people's.

On the other hand, when we become parents, we find ourselves preparing to ease our fledgling children out of the nest so that they can learn to fly. They need our support and encouragement as they gradually make their way in the world. And some of them may require this support for longer than others. We expect it to be that way. Independence requires varying degrees of interdependence.

So it is with people with learning disabilities. Some can be and are more independent than others. And, to the extent they can manage their own lives and affairs, this is desirable. But others need more support in order to live a fulfilling life. What is required from the rest of us is that they have the freedom to realise what for them will be 'life to the full'.

If we build this into our attitudes towards those with learning disabilities, we will find ourselves looking for possibilities rather than problems, bridges rather than barriers.

4 DIGNITY

Treating people with learning disabilities with respect is uncommon. The almost universal reaction is to treat them as children. The media encourage this by their fixation with mental age. We hear that Mary Smith, aged 22, has gone missing, and then we are told that 'she has a mental age of a five-year-old...' Immediately we know that this is a woman who is vulnerable. But, more than that, we think of her as childlike. Well, it may be that she has a reading age of a five-year-old, or that her vocabulary is no more than an infant's – but she has the life experience of a young adult. Whatever Mary's limitations, she is not a child.

It is at times embarrassing to hear people talking to adults who have a learning disability. The pitch of the voice rises; the language becomes babyish, the manner patronising – as if the speaker is somehow superior to the person she is speaking to. Many a young person with a learning disability is kept with little children in the Sunday School rather than joining her peers in the youth group. But those with learning disabilities should be treated in ways that are appropriate to their age and life experience. As adults, they should be encouraged to behave as adults, to dress as adults, to talk as adults, to be adults with adults.

5 INTEGRATION

For nearly two centuries people with learning disabilities were almost always separated from the rest of society and put into long-stay 'hospitals' for life. This policy of 'separate development' – more effective than apartheid was in South Africa – was a major contributory factor to the prevailing attitudes of hostility which still endure in society. Yet the fact that those with learning disabilities are people, like the rest of us, surely means that their proper place is among people. They are part of the community, and should be accepted and welcomed as such.

The idea of integration is fine in theory, but in practice it runs up against all sorts of prejudices. The 'not-in-my-backyard' outlook is typical. When a group of people with learning disabilities wants to live in our street, do we join the local protest? We might meet them in the corner shop! They might even show up in our church! However, the church is just where integration has to happen – even if it does challenge our traditional and conservative Christian culture.

6 SPIRITUALITY

No matter how much like the rest of the animal kingdom we may be at times, we humans are distinct in this respect – we have a soul. This is the essence of our humanity, breathed into our first parents by God in the very process of our creation. It follows that as the body has needs, so too does the soul. We are made for a relationship with God and cannot live satisfyingly without him. A relationship with God is as vital to us as food and drink are to the body. Sooner or later our need catches up with us and overtakes us.

If this is true for any of us, it is true for all of us – including those with learning disabilities. Everyone needs to hear about God's love for them, about the possibility of forgiveness through Jesus' death, about living a full life in the power of the Holy Spirit. Everyone needs to have the opportunity to become a part of the living Body of Christ in the world. If it is difficult to see how these things can be realised by people with learning disabilities, we must find and remove the barriers we place in their way. What we should not do is assume that they have no spiritual needs, or that those needs cannot be met. Rather, we must reflect on how they can take their intended place in the church and each make their unique contribution to its life.

Let's review where we are in our thinking. We have established that people are people because they are made in God's image, and that an enormous diversity exists among human beings. However, the fact that we find others more or less acceptable results from our personal culture – our social class, education, environment, family and the like. We have agreed (I hope!) a universal principle, incorporating six elements, which describes what gives people value, and we have applied that principle to people with learning disabilities. Or, to put it another way, we have acknowledged that humanness is what makes people beautiful.

Think it through

1   Human beings are God's special creation (Gen 1:26). What difference does this make to the way you understand other people? How ought this to influence your attitudes and behaviour towards them?

2 God created man and woman in his own image (1:27). In what ways do you perceive God's likeness in others? Are there any biblical grounds for saying that some people reflect God's image more than others?

3 'It is not good for the man to be alone' (2:18). Human beings are social creatures. How should this need be recognised and responded to in people with disabilities?

Chapter 2

Being different

Having agreed that people with learning disabilities are human beings, we can now ask what it is that marks them out from other human beings. In what ways are they different, and what causes those differences?

Definitions

It is almost impossible to arrive at a definition of learning disability which will be true of all the people to whom it might be expected to apply. Definitions tend to be influenced by the priorities of the person or organisation making them. So health organisations and trusts will define learning disability in terms of known medical characteristics or causes. An educationalist will define it in terms of intelligence, using IQ tests and tables to delineate disability as falling below a score of 70 and differing degrees of disability below that. The law offers its definitions as severe mental impairment and mental impairment, and refers to states of arrested or incomplete development of mind, impairment of intelligence and social functioning. And the sociologist will offer a definition where disability is decided in terms of the special services a person uses.

The standard definitions emphasise what people cannot do or be, and tell us very little about the person, their ability and their potential.

While we cannot neatly label every person with a learning disability, we can at least define some of the terms commonly used.

Impairment

This refers to difference (from the norm) that is a result of physical or brain-related factors. It leads to some loss of function intellectually or physically, or both.

Disability

The impairment disables the person so that he or she is restricted in some way. This generally relates to things most people are able to do or achieve – walking, talking, looking after one's self, for example. It may affect the person's ability to grasp ideas and concepts or to use acquired information.

Handicap

The society in which the disabled person lives is organised in such a way that his 'difference' becomes a handicap. For example, a person may be disabled by arthritis but he is handicapped by having to climb steps into the post office. A person disabled by brain damage is handicapped by having to read in order to claim a disability benefit.

Causes

> There is a story about a medical student who was taking his final oral examination and was answering all the questions very well indeed; he knew he was doing well. The professor was impressed and was almost finished. Then he said, 'Just one final question, Mr Johnson. What is the cause of Down's Syndrome?' The question worried the student because he did not want to end the examination in an unsatisfactory way. He hesitated and then answered, 'I'm sorry, professor, I did know but I have forgotten.' The professor looked at the student sadly and said, 'That's a great pity, Mr Johnson, because now nobody knows.'
>
> *B Stratford, Down's Syndrome:*
> *Past, present and future, Penguin, 1989.*

Only in a minority of cases can one identify a specific cause for learning disability. A survey in 1967 calculated that 70% of cases had no known cause. This percentage may have decreased a little but not much. Almost all forms of profound, severe or moderate learning disability are the result of some damage to or difference in the central nervous system, ie the brain. And most forms of damage or difference occur before, during or shortly after birth, though chromosomal or genetic abnormalities may occur at or soon after conception. The best known of these is Down's syndrome. We know what it is – having an extra chromosome 21. We know that it affects every cell in the body. We know that it is more likely to happen to parents who are older. We know that it affects around one in 650 babies, and that it has existed since ancient times. And we know that it results in widely differing degrees of ability and disability. But so far no one has been able to answer the question, 'What is the cause?'

Differences in genetic make-up result in 'neural tube defects', of which the best known is spina bifida. Over one-third of the children affected (one in every 500 live births) has a learning disability. Fragile X syndrome is thought to affect one in every 1,000 children.

It is more common in boys than girls, and is the result of an abnormal gene on the X chromosome. It too can cause widely different degrees of disability, and it is an inherited condition.

Over 2,000 single gene disorders have been identified and are thought to be responsible for around 10% of cases of severe impairment at birth. Autism has become more widely recognised in recent years but the mystery surrounding its cause, or causes, remains. Not all those affected by it have a learning disability, but all have serious difficulties in maintaining relationships.

Life in the womb, even for a healthy baby, is far from risk free. The mother's diet, health and habits will affect him or her for good or ill. If the mother contracts German measles in the first three months of her pregnancy, the risk of serious disability in the baby is high. Heavy smoking or drinking alcohol during pregnancy also risks indirectly causing learning disability in the baby.

During the birth process, a baby may suffer brain injury due to complications or oxygen starvation. Such injuries are thought to account for 10% of all cases of severe learning disability. In infancy, accidents (serious injury, or lead or mercury poisoning) and illnesses (meningitis and, to a lesser extent, whooping cough and measles) may also result in permanent disability.

To sum up then – profound, severe and moderate learning disability are the result of some damage to or difference in the central nervous system. The extent to which a child develops while having one of these conditions will be affected significantly by the extent to which he or she is accepted and assisted. Where a community loves and supports individuals with learning disabilities, their prospects are substantially better than where they suffer rejection or estrangement.

By now you will realise that it is impossible to give a one-sentence answer to the question, 'What are people with learning disabilities like?' My eldest daughter, Rachel (now in her thirties) is a gracious Christian lady. Mike is an aggressive, angry young man. Kate has a great love of life and remarkable skill in manipulating people. Mark is incredibly patient with me as I struggle to understand his nearly incoherent speech. In short, there is no answer to that question, anymore than there is to this one – 'What are *people* like?' Beauty is not about sameness.

Think it through

1 You now know a little about learning disability. Your general experience of life will also have informed you about mental illness. List some of the contrasts between the two – eg learning disability may cause stress, mental illness may be caused by stress – and surprise yourself at the way these two conditions are often confused!

2 Refer back to the Principle of Personal Value. How has what you have learnt about the causes of learning disability undergirded that principle?

Chapter 3

Being myself

We have now reached the third step in accepting people with learning disabilities. First, we accept them as people, acknowledging their place alongside us and extending to them the rights and responsibilities we wish for ourselves. Second, we accept their differentness, acknowledging that while their abilities may diverge from the average, they are able to contribute to the well-being of society as a whole. Maybe that's enough? Not quite.

Think for a moment about the way you relate to your bit of society. You take it for granted that you are 'normal', whatever that means. So you regard your interests and tastes as acceptable standards for other people. You find yourself itching to change those who differ widely from you, to make them 'normal' too! If you are a keen 'green', you will urge your friends to join Friends of the Earth or the local protest against a sewage works in the park. If you are a football fanatic, you may regard followers of cricket as dull. In fact, we each regard our divergent normality as desirable for other people, even though we usually accept that only a select band will be like ourselves!

This characteristic tends to become disproportionate when we meet people with learning disabilities: we see so many areas where improvement is, in our view, desirable. Their careless dressing, their out-of-tune singing, their too-loud 'Amens', their arriving too late (or too early), their overbearing hugs, their inadequate theology, their enthusiasm or indifference, their slurred speech, all draw from us the wish to 'improve' them. After all, we feel, they will be the beneficiaries.

Why not try coming from a different starting point when you get to know people with learning disabilities? Take time to see beyond your first impression, to discover who they really are, what they can do, what influences and experiences have shaped them. You will probably come to understand and admire the person you uncover, and be in a better position to discern whether or not improvement is possible or desirable.

Henry was a grown man with an almost obsessive concern for his mother. He would be perpetually asking how she was and repeatedly asking us to pray for her. He seemed unable to accept that God does not require endless repetition of our requests before he will respond. Eventually I learned that Henry's father had died while Henry was still a baby, and he had no brothers or sisters. For his mother, bringing Henry up alone in a high-rise council flat, life was an unending struggle. Now Henry lives in a residential care home, and she has grown old and frail with no one to turn to but her son. She shares all her worries with him in her weekly phone call. Henry will carry her burdens as best he can – she is, after all, the only person he has in the world – but, with his own severe learning disability, it is more than he can manage. However, I wonder if I would have coped as well as he has! Henry needs support from his friends, not earnest programmes to stop him asking pointless questions about his mother.

The same point could be made repeatedly. People with learning disabilities bear social disadvantages due to prejudice and fear for which we, rather than they, are responsible. They have to cope with these with their already limited resources. They need us to respond to them without preconditions, such as 'You must improve, or else!' We must search out their strengths and strengthen them further, rather than forever turning the spotlight of our anxiety on their weaknesses. This is no more than we ask our own friends to do for us!

Grace had a strange view of her future: she would never grow old and die. (Most people behave as if this were the case for them, but few admit to believing it.) A serious theological problem needed to be sorted out. Someone must put Grace right. Her Christian friends called me in. I needed to know from Grace what she was claiming for herself. It took quite a while of patient listening to understand what lay behind her strange conviction. It transpired that she had undergone major surgery as an infant some thirty years or more before. It was successful, and the surgeon had assured her that she was all right now – she wouldn't die. Nor had she, so far. Grace saw this in very simple terms, and it had long since been part of her outlook on life. What could I say to unravel this false view of herself and her future? It was not hard to decide – nothing! I felt that it was very unlikely I would change her point of view, based as it was on a lifelong misunderstanding of what she had been told. And, after all, it didn't really matter. Grace was ready for heaven, and at least she would have a pleasant surprise when she woke up and found herself there one day!

There is one change, however, that we must look for, and that is the spiritual transformation that follows conversion. The benefits which flow from this are incalculable, and we should settle for nothing less. But we must start where the person is, accepting him for who and what he is, bringing the love of God within the range of his awareness. The degree to which someone can express his understanding is not the measure of what he has grasped. The better we know him, the more we will perceive the progress he is making in his appreciation of God's care for him. Much will flow from our relationship.

Accepting people is not a special skill – you don't need a degree in psychology to achieve it. But accepting others is the fundamental prerequisite in *all* outreach and evangelism, whoever the target group happens to be. It is the first priority, no more nor less in respect of people with learning disabilities than of any other group of people.

Think it through
Use your imagination!
The residents of a newly opened residential home have attended three Sunday morning services. Some in the congregation think they are disruptive. Inappropriate behaviour has included:

- Constant shuffling or moving about.
- Sitting in the front and waving at people behind.
- Talking during prayers.
- Making clicking sounds, teeth-grinding.

As an elder you are charged by complainants to *do* something. Do you:

- Ask the home manager to stop the group coming to the services?
- Make clear to the group and to the staff, what the church's expectations of behaviour are?
- Offer help, so that their behaviour in church is improved?
- Adapt the church's culture to absorb the people with learning disabilities who attend?

See if you can come up with some specific proposals of what to do.

Part 2
APPROACHING

Those who have no contact with people with learning disabilities find it hard to believe they are present in such large numbers. On average, 2% of the population has a learning disability. This is about 1,200,000 in the United Kingdom – the same as the number of full-time students, a little less than the number of Asians in Britain (estimated at 1,500,000). However, people with learning disabilities seem far less in evidence than either of these other groups. Where are they?

It is true that you are less likely to bump into them in the high street than you are to see a student or an Asian. Indeed, you may not be able to remember meeting someone with a learning disability for a long time. They do live more sheltered and separate lives, but they are there in your community. Maybe it is a matter of knowing what to look for. I hardly ever go into town without seeing someone with a learning disability.

So large a group in society ought not to be overlooked by the church and, thankfully, there is evidence that past neglect is giving way to genuine concern and interest. The biggest questions churches face, and ask, are these:

- Where are they?
- How do we make contact?
- What can we do?

This section will start to provide answers.

Chapter 4
Setting clear goals

Let's start by being clear about what we are trying to achieve. What is our aim? We can be guided in this by considering the two great commandments:

> One of them, an expert in the law, tested Jesus with this question: 'Teacher, which is the greatest commandment in the Law?'
> Jesus replied: ' "Love the Lord your God with all your heart and with all your soul and with all your mind." This is the first and greatest commandment. And the second is like it: "Love your neighbour as yourself." All the Law and the Prophets hang on these two commandments.'
> *Matthew 22:35–40*

We are *commanded* to love our neighbour as ourselves. As we love others, we become an expression of God's love, and this is possible 'because *God has poured his love into our hearts by the Holy Spirit*' (Rom 5:5, my italics). It is an achievable aim (as well as a command) to bring God's love to people with learning disabilities, and to their families.

We now need to ask what this requires in practice. Three objectives spring naturally from such an aim:

- To build relationships with people with learning disabilities.
- To encourage their relationship with God.
- To develop their relationship with God's people, the church.

(If all this seems obvious, this is because we are thinking of those with learning disabilities as *people* first, people who happen to have a learning disability but whose primary need is to know God's love in their lives.) Let's take a closer look at these objectives.

Building relationships

More than half the people with learning disabilities in Britain live with their families. Many are children. We can assume that they live in more or less ordinary houses, in streets like your own. And, like the other people in your street, they would like neighbours who are neighbourly.

The level of fear and prejudice which still exists towards people with learning disabilities – at all ages – means that they feel isolated. Children often attend special schools, which means they are deprived of natural social contact and friendships with other children in their neighbourhood. They may continue at the same school from infancy right through their teens. At 19 years of age or so, they will probably transfer to full- or part-time attendance at an 'opportunity centre' of some sort. There they will continue to live more or less segregated lives.

The isolation of the child is likely to be shared by the family. Parents will have extra, ongoing demands made on their time and energy. They may well find themselves avoided by other parents who regard the differentness of their child an embarrassment. Any unusual behaviour on the part of the learning disabled son or daughter will deepen their isolation.

Adults with learning disabilities may have spent a lifetime in a long-stay institution, and have underdeveloped social skills. Their manners, or lack of them, may make for a hostile reception at the local pub. They may be dependent on a parent or member of staff to accompany them if they are to visit shops or community facilities – all of which traps them in their own narrow social circle.

God's love requires us to reach across the gulf that separates people with learning disabilities from our community, and to take the opportunity to develop friendships with them and their families. In other words, we simply need to do what should come naturally to us as Christians.

A relationship with God

Most of us want our friends to have firsthand experience of God's love and not just a second-hand experience through us. People with learning disabilities, like everyone else, are unavoidably disabled by unforgiven sin and spiritual blindness. We can do something about this by introducing them to the Saviour who died to forgive their sin and to bring them everlasting life.

But how can they get to know Jesus if the methods we use to communicate this good news actually compound their disability? If 'church' is the only route we offer, then we are building a fence across the 'narrow way' so far as people with learning disabilities are concerned. We expect our missionaries to master the language of the people they have been called to serve, so that they can effectively tell of God's love. We expect the evangelist to apply that message within a relevant cultural framework. The same principle applies for people with learning disabilities. We have to take account of their limitations so that when we present the gospel to them it will be within their grasp. To put it another way, we have to make what we say and do in church as accessible as we make the buildings themselves. It is not that this is difficult but rather that it requires us to be thoughtful and inclusive in our outlook.

Some may question whether people with learning disabilities understand enough of the gospel to become Christians. This is a vital issue to which we will give further thought later. In the meantime, let the experience of one man make its own point.

Dennis's behaviour became too difficult for his parents to manage, so he was sent to a long-stay institution. After some time he improved sufficiently to return home, though he still used the hospital day-centre every day. Some Christians invited Dennis to the local church, and he began to attend a Bible group run by Causeway PROSPECTS. His confidence grew as his contact with people widened. After a year or two Dennis

was converted. His parents noticed a difference in his attitudes and behaviour. Later he asked to be baptised. When asked for his reasons Dennis replied, 'Jesus is the best friend I've ever had.' Some time later Dennis shared some news in the Bible group: 'The hospital has said they don't want me any more. They say I'm too good for them.' Professionals had agreed that he had made so much improvement, he no longer needed their supervision. It is a story that could be repeated in one form or another many times over.

Integration into the Body of Christ

Evangelism has a church dimension. Every convert needs to become part of the Body of Christ so that he can learn how to work out his expanded awareness of God and himself on a day-to-day basis. The fellowship and example of others, along with the teaching ministry and worship of the church, will be part of this. So too will be the opportunity to express new-found life in service to others via the church, to give as well as to receive.

Becoming part of the Body of Christ is as necessary to the spiritual life and growth of a person with a learning disability as it is to anybody else. But for it to happen, the church needs to have teaching and worship that are appropriate, and to provide opportunities for them to express their love and faith among other believers. Is it too much to ask?

Not at all! As we have already seen, we have a God-given obligation towards people with learning disabilities simply because they are our neighbours in the community. This obligation is strengthened by the fact that, with few exceptions, most churches have hardly begun to realise that there is a need to be met, an opportunity to be taken. God will take responsibility for the outcome, be it success or failure. Ours is a duty of service.

Think it through

1 How much is your church – and how much are you – sensitive to the needs of people with learning disabilities? After your next attendance at a service, make a list of everything that happened to you from the moment you arrived until the moment you left. Include opening the door, shaking hands with the steward, *everything*. Then tick those items which would have been easy for someone with a learning disability, and put a cross by those which would have been difficult. What does this exercise show you?

2 Make a list of the ways in which your church is already responding to the needs of people with learning disabilities.

Chapter 5

Considering action

The passion for preaching as the supreme way of sharing the truth we have found in Jesus has long since gripped the church, especially its evangelical and evangelistic core. First a tract, then a testimony, then maybe a book, and then the full blown exposition of scripture, by which time the contact should be 'wowed' with our message and ripe for repentance and faith. Maybe it's the stuff of our dreams – and the other person's nightmare! Sharing the truth in this way is not for people with learning disabilities.

God's means of communicating his good news is rather different. First, there is incarnation – a being with, a coming among and alongside. Then there is the practical demonstration of concern for people, accompanied or followed by explanation. This ideal 'methodology' is beautifully expressed in Jesus. So, when we consider how to respond to the opportunity and challenge of people with learning disabilities in our community, we would do well to base our approach on this pattern. (Explaining how we communicate the truth will form Part 3 of this book.)

At home

At least 90% of children with learning disabilities are living at home as part of a family. Most attend special (state-funded) schools, but a small proportion benefit from mainstream education. Many more could do so with the right support – but that is another story.

It is estimated that about 40% of adults with learning disabilities also live with their families. The majority of these will attend a centre of some sort during the day. Demand exceeds supply of places, so their attendance may be less than daily. A small proportion of people with learning disabilities have ordinary jobs, although many have only part-time employment or work experience placements. The benefit system handicaps them when it comes to earnings – but that is yet another story.

In your parish or church district there will certainly be families supporting someone with a learning disability. They are likely to be open to someone prepared to take an interest in them. What issues are they likely to face?

WITH A CHILD

Depending on how they are given the news, parents are bound to find the fact that their child has a learning disability more or less devastating. In many instances they will be told soon after the baby is born, notably in recognisable genetic conditions such as Down's syndrome. The mother sometimes learns within hours of the birth that the baby she has nourished within her is 'not normal'. Her bundle of dreams falls apart in her arms and its place is taken by a lifelong burden, full of uncertainty. What she suffers is like a bereavement only worse; loss is only part of the picture.

For many parents, the realisation that their baby is different dawns slowly. As the child fails to reach the markers of natural development within the expected time-scale, a question mark turns into a question. The doctor, at first optimistic, begins to wonder. Then follow trips to a special clinic, special tests, special appointments, until eventually someone sad-faced and sombre tells them that their child has a learning disability. The same disappointment, the same sense of loss, of outrage or inner pain, and the same questions, questions, questions about the how, the why and the wherefore.

At such a time parents do not need clichés or false promises. They need understanding, patient help and, gradually, information about what to do, where to go, how to help. Some localities have voluntary welfare advisors, people who have made it their business to know about these things, whom the doctors can call in to give support, sympathy and advice. What an ideal role for a Christian!

It is probably too late to *start* helping the families already living around your church. They have already groped their way through that dark valley and are coping, to some extent, with the way things are. Think of some of the situations they face and how you could respond to them.

There are extra demands on a mother, compounded if she has other dependent children to care for. In infancy, there may be hospital visits which clash with the time another child must be collected from school or nursery; or problems with transport to and from a distant specialist clinic. When the child reaches school age, there may be waiting on a cold street corner for a coach to take her to a special school, perhaps at more or less the same time as another child must be taken to school elsewhere. And the coach is late, or it is raining! Supermarket shopping with children can be awful at the best of times, but becomes a nightmare if a child is hyperactive or grabs unpredictably at displays of piled-up tins!

Only a very little imagination is required to see such needs and to devise ways in which love can respond. But you don't know anyone affected? Keep your eyes open. Does a coach stop near your house and pick up youngsters every day? Did you see someone struggling in Tesco's with a child behaving strangely? Could you not stop and talk, find out a little more and then reflect as to whether you can offer help in the future? How often Madeleine wished she and Rachel had been invited to wait for the coach in a warm front-room nearby!

WITH AN ADULT

The first time we attended a local MENCAP meeting, Madeleine and I were struck by the fact that most of the parents there were well past middle age and their sons and daughters were adults. How, we wondered, do some of those older people cope with looking after their dependent adult? We are still wondering over thirty years later, even though we have often seen their courage, determination and commitment to care when other support should have been available long since.

For one mother I know, it was arthritis that put an end to her caring for her daughter: she simply could not support her in the bath any longer. The daughter had to go into a home miles from her friends and family. Her experience was marginally better than that of a young man who outlived his parents. Two days after his mother dropped dead in the kitchen, he called on his neighbour to complain that she was asleep on the floor and hadn't got his meals – two days of bewilderment, desolation and hunger.

The need for practical help which expresses love is self-evident in both instances. Every situation will vary in the opportunities it offers, but each one will, without question, provide occasion for the church, for local Christians, to incarnate God's love in practice.

IN THE FAMILY
Mention has already been made of the 'handicapped family', and the extent to which this occurs depends largely on people other than family members. Again, it is within the scope of the local church to make a difference. Natural contact with families which have children of similar ages is probably the most effective means of dispelling that sense of differentness. You might invite children with learning disabilities to parties, have the whole family round for a barbecue, encourage them to join your picnic – just everyday activities that make people feel they are being treated as normal.

Brothers and sisters of a child with learning disability may be disadvantaged through receiving less attention from parents than would otherwise be the case. A little attention from other families would cancel out that deficiency. Parents suffer too. Many lose any hope of being a normal couple, of being able to go out together from time to time because no one offers to babysit. The additional pressures on them may prove too much for their relationship – the level of family breakdown is said to be higher where there is a person with learning disability. It need not be inevitable!

What is needed to help families is so ordinary, so possible and yet so rare. Christians, more than most, have the resources of love, of social frameworks, of supernatural power, to make practical and helpful responses possible. It would not be surprising if they were pioneers in this field. In fact, the sad lesson of history is the opposite.

WITH THE AUTHORITIES
There is probably a bureaucratic response to almost every unusual family or personal situation. This is certainly so for learning disability. However, the systems change from time to time, varying from one area to another, and differing in extent and effectiveness so much that it is difficult to lay down clear guidelines as to what a family should do, where it should go or what it might expect from the state. For this reason, parents

of people with learning disabilities often give up trying, and miss out on the assistance, services or benefits which are there to help them and to which they have a right.

Churches often have among their number people who know the answers, or who know a man who does! A social worker, nurse, doctor or other professional can offer advice and point someone needing help in the right direction. A friend could accompany a mother on a visit to social services or the Department of Social Security, or speak up for her at a tribunal, or guide a father through the claim forms.

Love in practice.

In homes
If some 60% of people with learning disabilities don't live with their families, where do they live? We know that about 15,000 of them still live in long-stay institutions. The rest – the majority – live in homes in or near the community.

LOCAL AUTHORITY SERVICES
Since 1993, social services departments have been required to buy the services they need from private businesses or voluntary organisations. The changeover from local authority provision will take place progressively over the next few years. The local authority is also responsible for setting up a registration and inspection unit to approve and monitor the way these services are run. Residential care homes must be inspected at least annually and the reports published be made available to the public. 'Day opportunities' services are also provided or monitored by the local authority to ensure that people with learning disabilities have training and work opportunities. For financial reasons, services often fall short of being comprehensive.

HEALTH AUTHORITY SERVICES
Most of the long-stay institutions were run by health authorities. Some set up trusts which continue to provide for former residents in community-based homes. Many people with learning disabilities are in the care of charitable organisations, and some are in homes run by businesses. These may be funded by health authority sources.

VOLUNTARY SECTOR SERVICES
Historically, the provision of care and support for dependent groups of people has been the province of charities. There are many registered charities with familiar names working in this field: MENCAP, Home Farm Trust, CARE, Elizabeth Fitzroy Homes, MacIntyre and others. There are some which operate on Christian principles, both Protestant and Catholic: Shaftesbury, PROSPECTS (formerly A Cause for Concern), l'Arche, Walsingham Community Homes. Older charities tended to develop village communities outside of, but not far from, urban areas. In recent years the trend has been towards small, ordinary housing in the community.

PRIVATE BUSINESSES
Residential care for the elderly has been a growth industry, and in the field of learning disability it is probable that businesses undertake as many 'care contracts'

as charities. They are subject to the same rigorous standards and this has, thankfully, reduced the extent to which exploitation of people with learning disabilities can take place. Because economic priorities may apply in a commercial setting, there is a tendency for this sector to provide care in larger units with higher numbers of residents.

All services are expected to operate within a strategy developed by the local authority, which is regularly updated and available to members of the public.

Whichever 'type' of home you find in your area, there are likely to be certain features common to them all:

Tight staffing schedules

The biggest expense in running a home is staffing, and the greatest pressure on a home is to keep costs low. Inevitably, therefore, the organisation will keep staffing to the lowest optimum level. This will affect the extent to which staff can support residents in social (or spiritual) activities outside the home. This in turn makes voluntary help invaluable to staff and residents alike.

Limited life experience

Unless residents are capable of going out unaccompanied, they will either have to go in groups or not at all. So they will be seen by others as 'different', and have reduced opportunities to be an ordinary part of social life in the community.

These things being so, volunteers who befriend a person, spend time with him, take him to the pictures, invite him home, will be a treasure to home managers. The volunteer may have to undergo a police check to ensure they have no record of criminal activity or abuse, but that will surely not deter anyone who wishes to show and share God's concern for disadvantaged people.

This section has attempted to make some suggestions for action which are based on real-life situations and the needs that result from learning disability. It is unlikely they will apply to all situations, and they are certainly no more than pointers. Their purpose is to stir ideas, to alert you to the possibilities, to encourage you to start looking and thinking about the actual situation in your locality, to demonstrate that *something* can be done to bring hope and change to the people with learning disabilities, and their families, near you.

Think it through

1 In the space below, list anyone known to you who is connected to your church in any way and who has a learning disability.

2 List anyone known to you in your area who has a learning disability.

3 List anyone known to you in your church who works with people with learning disabilities.

4 Find out and list any local services available for people with learning disabilities, including special schools, day opportunity centres and residential homes.

Chapter 6

Making contact

Making a start

Begin where you are. Review the existing contacts the church has with people with learning disabilities, and their families. Is there a family in the church with a learning disabled child? How is that child provided for in the life of the church, in the Sunday School or the youth group? She may give you a point of contact with other families and individuals. Draw the family into discussion about other children known to them. What needs do they have which the church could meet? How can their child and her friends be integrated into the life of the church? What particular needs face them as a family in caring for their child, which the church could respond to?

There may be people with learning disabilities who attend church from time to time. They, their families (if they live at home) or the residential home where they live may also be a starting point of contact with others with learning disabilities.

There may be church members who work in local services for people with learning disabilities. They can provide an introduction to the manager of their service, so that ways of helping can be explored. They may also be able to give information about other local services and organisations.

If you have neither contact nor knowledge of where to go, you need to do some research. There are two distinct avenues open to you.

1 Approaching local or national organisations

You might contact an organisation which supports families of people with learning disabilities. The best known and most widespread is MENCAP. MENCAP has local branches all over the country, and some of these are very aware of what is happening in their area. There are others for specific disabilities, and they may have different members from the MENCAP group. (See 'Resources' on p 53 listing the national headquarters of various organisations which can put you in touch with their local representatives.)

2 Researching reports

Reports on organisations and services for people with learning disabilities are available through the social services department or the local library's reference section. Reports on inspections of residential care homes are also available for you to see. These will give you the address and phone number of the office and name of the manager. Some areas publish directories of services for people with learning disabilities.

Making contact

You will probably find that you acquire more information than you can act upon! At this point, pause. You can't reverse years, centuries even, of indifference in twenty-four hours! And you can't address the whole field of need. It is as well to gather a group of Christian friends, or to go to your church prayer meeting and pray for wisdom. What response should you and your church make to what you now know?

One thing more before you lay your plans – can you keep it up? The people on whom you intend to call may receive your offer with a 'We've been here before' smile. And not without reason. Many people with learning disabilities have been disappointed by the speed with which their enthusiastic visitor runs out of time and commitment. Be sure you won't give them another occasion to feel let down. If you are to succeed, you must win the trust and confidence of both the carer and the person with a learning disability. This may take time – more time, if your first contact is about some big scheme, untried and unproven.

John was sure he had to do something for a nearby home for people with learning disabilities. He was scared stiff, completely inexperienced in contact with disabled people. Maybe he could do some shopping for the home, help with washing up, or something else…

'I have just the job for you,' said the manager, smiling. 'Come and see Brian every Thursday evening – before *The Bill*, mind.' John felt the blood drain from his face. It was not what he had expected or offered, or felt was his mission. But he went, at first almost speechless with tension. He left feeling a complete failure. And it went on like this for weeks. Then, gradually, he was able to relax with Brian and understand him.

John got to know others in the home. Eventually he asked the manager about taking Brian out, and then to church, and then to a Causeway Group. In time, several others attended with him.

Approaching people with learning disabilities as individuals, and taking time to get to know them, will uncover some surprising things. I discovered that the ugliest face I had ever seen became quite radiant when she smiled. I found that the most difficult speech I had ever struggled to listen to became fluent when he sang the praise of Jesus. I discovered gentleness, kindness, thoughtfulness, meekness, where I had never looked before. Beauty beyond mere external appearances became increasingly apparent as I got to know people with learning disabilities.

Think it through

1 Work out a process for making contact with people with learning disabilities, and their carers.

2 Plan a strategy for integrating people with learning disabilities into the life of your church. If you think you have done rather well, share your strategy with your church leader!

Part 3
TELLING

The story so far

We have seen that we are under an obligation to show God's love to our 'neighbour', and we have recognised that this includes people with learning disabilities.

We have seen that people with learning disabilities, and their families, have needs to which we can respond. Our church life tends to create barriers; we need to ensure that we are welcoming and accessible if we are to invite them to share in it.

We have set out some objectives as to what we can do to express God's love. There are practical possibilities which we can explore in diverse local situations. However, helpful as it is to alleviate loneliness, kindle hope or encourage a sense of community, these things may still leave untouched the spiritual need that lies deep inside every human being.

Sooner or later we must explain what we are doing. We need to communicate that it is God's love which motivates us, and not just that we are 'nice people'. Not only this: we must also tell them about Jesus. Hearing about him is essential to salvation: 'How can they believe in the one of whom they have not heard?' (Rom 10:14).

It is very natural for us to think in terms of inviting people to church. However, our Sunday services are for the whole congregation and cannot realistically be adapted to the needs of only one group within it. People with learning disabilities who attend must be considered and, in view of the obstacles we create, some means must be found to ensure that they receive benefit from being present. But their specific needs require specific ministry – ideally, in separate, regular meetings which supplement the Sunday services. These might be held two or three times a month, on a weekday evening. The rest of this book is about how to develop and run such meetings.

Chapter 7

Principles

Conversion is possible

We have already touched on the question, 'Can people with learning disabilities understand enough to be converted?' Whether this is a matter for debate in theologically 'sound' circles, or of sincere concern for those involved in the practical care for such people, the suspicion is the same – that we set people up to fail by encouraging them to help those with learning disabilities to become Christians. This is a profoundly important issue.

Some ask the question because they feel that people with learning disabilities may not need to be converted – they are innocent (just ask for a parent's opinion on this!) or somehow covered by the death of Jesus, and therefore do not need to respond. Others say that they are saved unless they knowingly say 'No' to God. These suggestions might appear to solve our difficulties, but in fact they compound them.

Are people with learning disabilities exempt from what scripture says about human beings in general? And, if so, we might ask how disabled must a person be for this exemption to apply? Where is the line of demarcation?

The Bible does not seem to say anything specific on this issue, but surely what it does say about human nature, sin and salvation applies no less to people with learning disabilities than to the rest of humanity. We see in them the same characteristics, the same weakness, the same tendencies to self-centredness and sinfulness that we find in ourselves. And in those who have become Christians we see as much evidence of compassion, kindness and holiness as in other believers.

The nub of the issue is what happens at conversion. What is it that makes a person a Christian? Is it having a sufficient degree of knowledge and understanding of what God has done for us through Christ? Scripture and experience point in a different direction. Many of us were slow to accept God's love in Christ even when we were reasonably well-informed on the subject. We were familiar enough with the Bible to know we were sinful and only Jesus could forgive our sins. But we remained unwilling to commit ourselves to him in faith – until the Holy Spirit worked in our lives. 'Regeneration' is the key event: Jesus told Nicodemus that he needed to be reborn (John 3:1–21); in Ephesians 2, Paul describes the process as being made alive. Only through regeneration does someone come to life in Christ, regardless of ability or disability, knowledge or ignorance.

It is this that gives point and purpose to ministry

among people with learning disabilities. They can know God because God can and does reveal himself to them (eg Luke 10:21). The ability of the person to tell us what has happened to them, to articulate or rationalise their experience, does not determine whether or not it is real in them.

How do we know whether or not a person with a learning disability has become a Christian? Jesus said, 'By their fruit you will know them' (Matt 7:16). An enjoyment of God's family is one indicator (1 John 3:14); a change in behaviour is another. Different priorities, a desire to pray, a concern for others…

Perhaps it is particularly important to apply such tests to people with learning disabilities. They love to please those they like, and it is not difficult to persuade them to accept what we say. Our motivation should not be to increase our count of converts but, rather, to ensure that they know direct enjoyment of God's love and care.

Truth is essential

'Isn't it rather like Sunday School?' The implication is that teaching adults with learning disabilities must be rather like teaching children. Not so! One of the aims of Sunday School is to provide a good base of Bible knowledge for children. Most of us associate the stories of the Old Testament with memories of Sunday School, perhaps with a particular teacher, and we are grateful for that knowledge. But ministry to people with learning disabilities must be more than just telling them Bible stories. It must be concerned with teaching truth in a way that can be understood and applied in their lives. However, this presents us with a problem. Truth is abstract. It is about concepts and ideas. As this is a major area of impairment for people with learning disabilities, the challenge is to find effective ways to communicate truth to them so that they are able to receive it.

It is as though we were walking along a narrow causeway with a swamp on either side – storytelling on the one hand and abstract concepts on the other. Madeleine has already groped her way across that causeway, getting a muddy foot from time to time. Countless others have followed the path she trod, and have used what she has developed out of her experiences for the benefit of hundreds, even thousands of people with learning disabilities in Britain and overseas. The methods and teaching material in this book is a result of many years' direct ministry to people with a wide range of learning disabilities. You can have confidence in it.

Teaching must be clear

In my own experience, preparation for ministry to people with learning disabilities is at least as demanding as that required to address a large and able congregation. It is a stricter discipline, with no room for woolliness or waffle! Not only must one be concerned about what one wants to say but also about how to say it.

MAKING A POINT

One point, and one point only, is enough for a good sermon. So taught Dr Kevan, the first principal of the London Bible College, advising his students that after preparing a sermon they should write its message in a single sentence. We would be wise to follow his advice when speaking to those with learning disabilities, limited as they are in their ability to move from one theme to another.

SPEAK THEIR LANGUAGE

A person with learning disability is likely to have a more or less limited vocabulary. Unless they have grown up in a Christian family, it is unlikely to include Christian terminology. Even if it does, they may still not understand what such terminology actually means. So jargon is out – and not only obvious words like 'sacrifice' or 'atonement', but also the quaint phrases we often use, such as 'Let us come to God in prayer'. Why not 'Let us pray' or, better still, 'Let us talk to God'?

Simplicity in language is essential for clear communication with those with learning disabilities. Strangely, many people find this very difficult: it's as if they had to learn a new way of thinking and speaking. To overcome this, it may be helpful at first to write down what you want to say in your introduction to the meeting, or in the talk you are about to give, and establish what songs and prayers you want to use beforehand. Then you will be able to check that the language is appropriate.

Simplicity in communication may seem to present a particular difficulty when it comes to Bible reading, but there are now translations available which are much clearer for people with learning disabilities. The best is the *Easy to Read* version, which uses short sentences and replaces pronouns with proper names. When a technical word is unavoidable, like 'synagogue', there is an explanation at the foot of every page where this occurs. (See 'Resources' for more information.) The team should agree on the version to be used, and all speakers should comply, so as to avoid confusion.

METAPHORS AND THE LIKE

Our rich language provides us with vivid similes and metaphors. We use them in ordinary conversation. They provide a source of lively illustrations for speakers and preachers, making their talks easier to remember. Jesus' ministry was enriched by his use of parables. So it is somewhat unnerving to discover that what we think of as aids will actually render our ministry to those with learning disabilities more difficult. The process of 'translation' necessary to make metaphors, similes, symbols and parables meaningful is highly sophisticated: as a general rule, it is beyond the ability of people with learning disabilities. So we might speak of Jesus as the light of the world and illustrate what we say with a candle, but they may then conclude that Jesus *is* a candle!

Madeleine once attempted to teach from the 'I am… sayings of Jesus – 'I am the door', 'I am the bread of life', 'I am the good shepherd', and so on. After the first lesson she came home very discouraged – she knew she had failed. She made a second attempt, giving far more thought to 'translating' the picture in ways that would really relate to her friends with learning disabilities. This time she was successful, but only by dint of very careful and applied teaching.

DON'T FORGET APPLICATION

People with learning disabilities live outside the mainstream of life. They use special services that the rest of us may never see. To make our teaching applicable to their way of life, we will have to become familiar with their world. This will involve visiting them in their residential care homes, attending open days at their opportunity centres, serving as volunteers at their clubs, so that we see for ourselves how things work, what opportunities and limitations they experience, how they and others in their world relate to one another. And we must then reflect on how their faith, hope and love can be expressed in those settings.

BE FLEXIBLE

A group of people with learning disabilities will vary in even more ways than the average congregation. Within a single meeting you may have someone who can read sitting alongside someone who cannot talk. You may have those who can listen for ten minutes and those for whom one minute is too long. Most are happy to sit quietly, but one may want to walk about while another wants to make sounds all the time.

Those who teach and lead a group of people with learning disabilities must be ready to adapt what they do and say so that the whole group can benefit. Helpers may be needed to assist along the way so that those who are more severely disabled receive what is shared in smaller bites and even simpler terms. Physical disturbances may mean that the talk has to stop for a bit and everyone sings a song while the disturber settles down again. Flexibility is the key to effectiveness.

Think it through

Write a short explanation of how you became a Christian as you might tell it to someone with a learning disability. Take care to use simple language, to explain the concepts and contexts, and to avoid metaphors and similes. Try reading it to a friend, telling him to interrupt you if there is anything he considers too hard for people with learning disabilities to understand.

Chapter 8

PRACTICE

By now you are, I hope, willing to think about *doing* something. I'm assuming that this is so, and will take you by the hand to help you get started. Don't be shy! This could be the beginning of an exciting new phase in your Christian life and service. If you feel unsure of yourself, here are some certainties to encourage you:

- God is very pleased that you share his concern for disadvantaged people.
- People with learning disabilities, and their families, will be pleased that you show concern for them.
- The Holy Spirit will help you in what you do for people with learning disabilities. He can make you equal to the task: God 'has made us competent as ministers of a new covenant' (2 Cor 3:6).

This section will explain what to do and give you the tools you need, or tell you where to find them. If this book has inspired you to get involved, gather together a group of interested friends to discuss and pray over what might be done. What follows will give you guidance on running a series of meetings, and provide session material and teaching samples. You can stick to it like glue or use it as a launch-pad to send you into orbit!

People first

This is not something you can do on your own! You will need help from the right sort of people. Before doing anything else, you should build up a team who can assist you. Who should you be looking for?

At the outset it is wise to find people you know, who share your outlook and faith. You don't want the project to collapse because of protracted discussions and arguments on points of doctrine which have nothing to with your intended activity. If possible, make it a local church project, drawing on other members of your own fellowship. Once the team has been established and the ministry is under way, others can be invited to assist, thereby widening the contacts and the ministry.

As you look for recruits, your attention will be drawn to the gifted and already over-committed members of the church. If they can help, well and good, but don't restrict your search to them. There are people in most congregations who are under-used but who have gifts of friendship and helpfulness you will find invaluable.

QUALITIES IN THE TEAM
- *Genuine concern* that people with learning disabilities should understand and experience God's love for them; that they should become Christians and develop as Christians.
- *Sensitivity* – aware of and responsive to the needs, moods and concerns of others.
- *Patience* – able to go at the pace of the person who seems slow to understand or respond; a willingness to rejoice at progress in small stages.
- *Love* – which sees more than the awkward movements, which hears more than what is poorly expressed, which values smiles; or, to express it differently, which shows the fruit of the Spirit (Gal 5:22).

- *Stickability* – people who won't give up after the first three meetings, who will be with you this time next year and the year after!

Skills in the team

Those who already work with people with learning disabilities seem an obvious choice. Their skills as nurses, carers or teachers will be valuable. However, it is *essential* that they share the team's concern for the spiritual welfare of your group. It is also desirable that they do not behave as though they are 'the experts.'

No one person need have all the skills, but among the team members the following qualities will be required:

- The ability to make truth clear in simple language.
- The ability to lead worship meaningfully using simple language, and to play musical instruments (no limit on number or variety!).
- The ability to cope with unusual behaviour.

Attitudes in the team

Patronising attitudes are unhelpful and must be avoided at all costs. You will be dealing with people who may be illiterate but not necessarily unintelligent, whose experience of life is the same as their age, who should be regarded with respect as well as affection.

Training

It really is worth spending time together as a team, working through this book, doing the studies and exercises. This will help you develop a shared understanding and an agreed approach to issues. Once you are up and running, plan the occasional evening to review the previous session or to plan the next one. And Causeway PROSPECTS can provide regular training in different parts of the country.

People to participate

You need people with learning disabilities to attend, obviously! We have already seen that they are in the community, and we have looked at how they may be contacted. There may be individuals with learning disabilities attending your church, whose families are members. Why not begin a group for them first and, once it is established and your team has more confidence, expand it to include others?

People with learning disabilities may be attending services from a local residential home. Before inviting them to join a special group, approach the home's manager to discuss your proposals. You may need to convince professionals that you have a genuine interest in their clients, that you want to involve them in the community and that you are not out to exploit or brainwash them! This should not be difficult if you have already established contact through voluntary work.

Your local branch of MENCAP may be willing to circulate its members. The Gateway Club may let you visit and talk to those who attend. Other associations may be willing to cooperate. Again, active involvement as volunteers will open doors. Personal approaches will be most effective.

A place to meet

You will need a light, warm and comfortable room with enough space for people to move around easily. It should be a pleasant room to be in – if possible, well-lit with attractive decor and comfortable chairs. If your church doesn't have such a room, ask permission to convert the draughty church hall (or part of it) into a lounge! At least make use of posters on drab walls.

The meeting place must be warm – many people with learning disabilities have poor circulation or limited mobility, and if they are cold you won't achieve much! A ground-floor room is essential for anyone in a wheelchair, and older people may also find stairs difficult. And, of course, it will help to have toilets nearby.

As far as possible, use the same venue for each meeting, to give those coming a sense of security. It is wise to have the room ready before the meeting, and every member of your team available to welcome people and help them to settle. If you are moving chairs or setting up the screen, you will cause distraction and confusion. Some music playing as they come in will cover awkward silences or give a focus for conversation. Whatever you do, avoid having them waiting outside in the cold because team members are late!

Anybody coming to a strange place and meeting strange people finds the experience bewildering. So, in early meetings, spend time on introductions and 'getting to know you' sessions. If someone has difficulty speaking, find out her personal details from her carers so that she can be prompted and others helped to understand. Give her time to express herself – other disabled people will be much more tolerant of communication problems than you are! Try to allocate a team member to a small group for an agreed number of meetings. Then change around so as to mix team and group members.

Running a meeting

Start by regarding the meeting as an informal Christian gathering with people with learning disabilities; this will help set the right atmosphere. It is not a 'service', though it may have many of the usual elements of a service. It is not something the team will do to or for people with learning disabilities. It is a meeting in which together everyone will approach, praise and learn from God.

It is the responsibility of the person leading the meeting to help everyone feel part of what is happening. While some may take a more prominent role, all should be free to participate. And there will be certain key elements.

Welcome

Everybody should feel welcome, especially those who have been absent for a while or who are attending for the first time. Names are important, so learn and use them. (If, like me, you forget names quickly, apologise and ask again!) Addressing people by name, particularly from the front, will help them feel significant and valued.

Worship

This is a vital part of the meeting and, with thoughtful planning, can reinforce the theme and the message of the session as a whole. The worship leader and the person doing the teaching could meet and plan each meeting together beforehand.

Songs and music

In most churches, worship has changed considerably in the last twenty years. We may regard this with mixed feelings, but for people with learning disabilities it is a distinct advantage to have user-friendly material that is less dependent on the ability to read and appreciate Victorian poetry!

However, modern songs can be as rich with biblical allusion and metaphor as those of older generations. We sing about trees clapping, chains breaking, knees bowing, heaven declaring, deer panting, and so on. All wonderfully worshipful – if you understand it! Thankfully, simpler songs, many of which allow repetition, are now available in large numbers and great variety. Some have been specially written for use by people with learning disabilities.

Words and concepts need to be explained. 'I'm accepted…' may need to be made clear. Word pictures like 'the Lamb', 'the Throne' and 'Our God reigns…' (which may be confused with poor weather!) will mean more if they are described clearly from time to time.

Use an overhead projector and screen. Books require numeracy as well as literacy! Causeway PROSPECTS produces a 'words only' song book containing 70 recommended songs, using different coloured paper for each page. Even if members are poor (or non-) readers, recognising some words will increase their confidence as they sing. Spend time teaching the songs. Try saying the words of each line together before singing a verse. The worship leader could speak out the words of the next phrase as people are singing.

Having more than one musician will be an advantage. Create some 'spaces' during worship where the instruments play and the group just listens. This will give them the opportunity to relax their limited concentration. Periods of silence may also be helpful.

Prayer and praying

'Talking to God' must be made a meaningful part of every meeting. Encouraging people with learning disabilities in prayer requires example and participation. God has no difficulty understanding a person's heart. Unclear speech or limited language must be seen as OK.

Be flexible in how prayer is used. Periods of silent prayer require a high level of concentration, so give clear guidance during the silence. Small groups, including a team member in each group, will become popular once members become used to each other.

There may be a tendency to copy each other, which can be helpful. If it proves not to be, help individuals to move on in prayer themselves. Some may make the same requests meeting after meeting. This may be very positive: 'Lord, I want to know you better.' It may also be rather limiting: 'Please bless my mum and dad, my brother and his family. Bless Aunty Mary…' Sensitive encouragement to move on will be required on a one-to-one basis.

Be alert to people carrying the burden of bereavement long after a parent has died. 'Please pray for my mum – she died last year' signals the need for help in coming to terms with loss. Start where the bereaved person is, and pray for him in his sadness. Over several meetings, it may be possible to help him cope with unexpressed grief. Be patient. People with learning disabilities have often been dealt with unhelpfully when bereaved, and may require repeated reassurance and help.

Movement and action

Even if members come from conservative church backgrounds, they will readily enter into physical expressions of worship. Clapping will help to show their joy; embraces will show their care for one another. Some will just about manage this; others may find even this difficult. But it is a wonderful thing to see a person who has been silent and motionless in worship begin gently to tap their foot or quietly clap their hands. These seemingly modest responses may be the outward expression of a genuine sense of gratitude and love for God.

Worship leading

The example set by the worship leader will have a significant influence. Her tone of voice should express sincere and joyful love for the Lord so that those listening will be encouraged in their own faith and love. If a song used is a prayer – eg 'Holy Spirit, come to me I pray' – explain what may happen as God answers that prayer.

Use songs that reinforce teaching and explain the link. 'God is our Father' is very helpful in making our relationship to God clear.

PARTICIPATION

People with learning disabilities (like the rest of us) learn best by doing. There are various points at which it will be possible to encourage those in your group to participate during the 'worship' time and the teaching. Leaders will be able to assess, after a few meetings, how to make the most of this.

It is wise to give specific times for sharing news and concerns. If someone wants to tell the rest of the group something (anything! – well almost), give them time. Encourage people with learning disabilities to support each other in this. If a person is worried about an issue, ask someone else to pray for him, then and there.

Some may wish to lead singing at some point. A more able person could be asked (and helped, if necessary) to read a few verses of scripture. If one of the group is converted, he may want to tell everyone. People with learning disabilities are not usually given the dignity of taking a leading role. It is worth watching out for ability in this area so that individuals could share the 'up front' responsibility.

Another opportunity for participation may arise during the teaching. The concentration span of the listeners is probably quite short. It can be helpful, therefore, to interject teaching with questions. Those who have answered questions or supplied information will feel good about it and want to listen to what you say next. Wrong answers should not be accepted as correct, but don't humiliate those who get it wrong.

Teaching

PREPARATION

Careful preparation is the key to an effective ministry to people with learning disabilities. With only ten minutes for the talk, each minute is absolutely vital. The central principles to follow are these:

- *Have a clear objective.* What single thing do you want to convey to the group? Decide what this is, and be sure that you get it across. Be content with achieving one goal only.
- *Be careful about concepts.* Abstract ideas are the stuff of preachers – and the stuffing of hearers! Root what is said in narrative.
- *Repeat yourself!* Not by mindlessly using the same words, but by constructively developing one theme in various ways, meeting after meeting.
- *Watch your language.* Jargon words are unhelpful – they may be familiar but misunderstood. Even everyday words may require explanation: 'God has plans for your life' might, for example, be approached through a conversation about planning holidays.
- *Be relevant.* Relate what is taught to people's real-life experiences.

PRESENTATION

The person speaking will be addressing adults. They may have a reading age of a six-year-old but be in their mid-twenties with as many years' life experience. Reflect this in the way you speak to them.

Use different approaches from one meeting to the next. Dramatise a narrative, or tell the story as if you were an eye-witness. Be careful to make clear that you are pretending (or they may think you are very old!). Find ways to involve them in what you are trying to convey. Where crowd scenes are being described, the whole group can be involved.

Role-play may be helpful for some, as are visual aids – but don't over-use them. It would be better to ensure a dynamic narration of an incident than to rely on a picture. Illustrations may confuse rather than help, and the flannelgraph approach can seem childish. Find exciting ways of using visual aids – for example, using a video recording of crowd scenes from the news will help convey an impression of the number of people fed with five loaves and two fishes.

Maps need to be explained. The group may require help to understand what they are. Unless it is a relief map, describe the terrain – hilly, valley, desert. Make overhead-projector slides of maps, and explain them in relation to the area in which the group lives. For example, if you are using a map that shows how far Bethlehem is from Jerusalem, talk about walking to a known location about the same distance from the meeting place.

TAKE-HOME PAPERS

It is useful to provide some form of 'take home' material: this will inform carers and help them follow up what you have been teaching. Encourage group members to ask someone to read the take-home material to them if they can't read it themselves. And provide a folder or wallet in which they can keep their papers.

Difficulties

You may be feeling that there must be a snag somewhere. It can't be as easy as I have made out! Well, it can be. It all depends on those taking part. To assume that people with learning disabilities invariably bring problems in their wake is unfair. But situations may arise which require a response from you and the team. What sorts of things could happen? We will consider a few of the more common ones. But remember, every situation will be different. There are no pat answers.

ATTENTION SEEKING

John remained in his place at the end of the meeting. He was crying quietly. When asked what was wrong, he seemed to say that he wanted Jesus to forgive him. You can imagine how the enthusiastic helper would respond. But more or less the same thing happened after the next meeting. And the next...

When the helper began to be firm with John, he asked for another team member whom he expected to be more understanding. The team decided to ignore John when this happened, but he took to more dramatic strategies like lying, sobbing, on the floor.

The team then decided that in future they would make an effort to talk to John when he arrived at meetings and to support him during the session, giving him attention in a more acceptable manner. His behaviour soon changed, and his former chirpy character emerged again.

Everyone needs attention. We all need to be noticed, valued, appreciated by others. We employ subtle and sophisticated skills to achieve this – body language, turns of phrase, facial expressions, not to mention clothes, make up and hair style. People with learning disabilities often suffer rejection and the experience of being devalued and disregarded. We should not be surprised if they try to change things! Our response needs to be one of valuing them while not giving in to the pressure of their demands.

PERFORMANCE

Mildred wanted to do the Bible reading. She was welcomed to the front to share her favourite verses. However, it quickly became apparent that she could not actually read, and was making up what she was saying as she stared at the pages of her open Bible. The leader thanked her as she took her seat. At the next meeting Mildred wanted to read again. She was allowed to repeat her charade because no one wanted to upset her.

There are two lessons to learn here. First, we must not elevate skills which are uncommon among people with learning disabilities so that those who lack them feel second-class. Reading, after all, is not that important. The majority of human beings throughout history have been illiterate. Develop an atmosphere in meetings which makes reading no more important than the skill of washing your face! Second, we should not play games with people. Mildred may be able to lead in prayer or choose the songs for the meeting. Discover her gift and encourage it to blossom, but help her to understand that if she cannot read she still has your respect and affection.

'TANTRUMS'

There may be the occasional outburst that disturbs the meeting, possibly through anger or a reaction to something. More likely, it relates to an incident that occurred before the meeting – a distressing phone call, or anxiety because a parent is in hospital. It may be the unfamiliar setting, or some pain that the person cannot describe.

If the person has come alone, a helper should offer to accompany him on a short walk outside the room and try to discover what the worry is, gently seeking to quieten his agitation. If the person wants to stay in the meeting room, whoever is leading should do something to absorb the distress, like having a short time of singing. If the incident recurs, ask the advice of carers: they may be able to advise on how to respond. But make it clear that you are not wanting to exclude the person.

CONVULSIONS

Many people with learning disabilities have epilepsy. Though this is usually well controlled by medication, some first-aid training should be given to helpers so that they know how to respond in the event of a person having a fit. Carers will usually inform the team if there is any likelihood of difficulty.

There are forms of behaviour which simply have to be accepted and tolerated. They are part of the individual and began way back in childhood. These would include obsessional behaviour or unwitting habits that are more or less involuntary. Grinding teeth, grunting, finger touching, ritual hand movements, rocking to and fro all come into this category. Accepting someone means accepting them as they are and for what they are.

Evaluation

The team will quickly develop into an effective group if they pause from time to time to review their efforts, particularly in the early weeks. The quality of what happens in the group can be improved by making an honest appraisal of the meetings. Initially, review each meeting as soon as possible after the conclusion. Be encouraging and honest! Here are some suggestions of issues to consider.

WHAT DID IT FEEL LIKE?

Look at the setting you used:

- Was the temperature comfortable?
- Was the seating sufficiently informal?
- Was the setting attractive enough?

Look at relationships:

- Was everyone welcomed?
- Would people have felt supported?

- Did you have enough helpers?
- Did people with learning disabilities relate to team members, and to others with disabilities?

WHAT ABOUT THE WORSHIP TIME?

The use of music can be so valuable – if you get it right!

- Was the music at the right volume?
- Were the songs played at the right pace for the people present? (Fast may be fun, but hard to sing to!)
- Are more/better musicians needed?

Aim to involve everyone in the singing.

- How effective was your introduction to the songs?
- How easily did people pick up the words?
- How well did they join in the singing?

PARTICIPATION

- Was there any?
- Was there too much?
- How could this be improved at the next meeting?

REVIEW THE TEACHING

Don't be too hard on the teacher – it may be your turn next time!

- Did people listen well?
- Was the 'lesson' too long/short?
- Was the language simple enough?
- Would any 'indirect' teaching method (eg drama) have made things clearer?

RESPONSES AND REACTIONS

- Were questions answered?
- Were any comments made by those with learning disabilities, which showed what they had received?
- If you had a learning disability, would you want to come again?

Think it through

1 Choose two songs or hymns which are sung regularly in your church. Work out how you would explain their meaning to a person with a learning disability. Look for words and concepts which, while familiar to us, may be obscure to them or simply incomprehensible. What would you need to say to help them sing the song meaningfully?

2 A person with a learning disability asks to be baptised as a believer. What criteria should be applied to assess whether or not it is right to agree to their request? Clue: the answer is not complicated!

CONCLUSION

Now it's over to you. My hope is that what you have read will have stirred up an interest in and concern for people with learning disabilities, or have strengthened the concern you already feel. At the very least you now know more about the issues, and the Bible repeatedly links knowing with doing. This was not intended as an educational trip: you have been targeted to do something!

Let me offer some reassurance. I frequently hear Christians saying how worthwhile they found it to become involved with people with learning disabilities. One vicar said that forming a Causeway PROSPECTS group was the most enriching thing the church had done in years. A church leader reported that their Causeway PROSPECTS group was the fasting growing aspect of the church's life. Numerous Causeway PROSPECTS group leaders have said that it has been the most spiritually fulfilling activity they have ever been part of.

I have tried to analyse why people react in this way. So far I am not satisfied with the answers. Perhaps it is the uncomplicated, unsophisticated and open response of people with learning disabilities, which challenges those of us involved. There is so often a simplicity that goes to the heart of matters, setting aside the precision of our theological stances or ecclesiastical dogmas to revel in love for Jesus and his family. But lacking the explanation does not diminish the joy of just sharing the unthreatening, accepting love of God for and through people with learning disabilities.

God bless you as you share the experience.

Part 4

TEACHING

What this section contains

I am assuming that those using this book have never before been involved in meetings for people with learning disabilities. Here you should find everything you need to run one effectively. There are nine sessions in all – so, at two meetings a month, this manual should serve for at least four months – and the 'help' level decreases as you go through the sessions. You should gradually discover what works for your particular group, and develop your meetings from there.

At the end of the book are sheets for group members to take home, which can be photocopied, and you may use these along with the one on p 55 to create your own group news-sheet. Numbers of the songs included in the programmes are given as they are found in *Mission Praise* (MP, the combined words edition) and *Songs of Fellowship* (SOF), or they can be obtained from Causeway Music (CM).

On pp 53–54 there is a list of resources, with details of a series of teaching packs (also available from Causeway PROSPECTS) which aim to develop further the understanding of the concept of God. Causeway Music songbooks and tapes, and the *Easy to Read* version of the Bible, are also mentioned. Additional tape recordings of the teaching given to people with learning disabilities at Spring Harvest can be obtained from Causeway PROSPECTS. These may be used in training or given to people with learning disabilities to listen to at home. The Resources section includes organisations involved with learning disability, not all of which are Christian. Some may be able to provide information about learning disability or about services provided for people with learning disabilities in your area.

Preparing yourself

All team members play a vital role in bringing God's word to people with learning disabilities. It is crucial that they prepare their own hearts and minds for the ministry they undertake. Jesus said, 'Out of the overflow of the heart the mouth speaks' (Matt 12:34). If they prepare only their minds, by studying the material here, all they will communicate is information. To be a channel of God's life and love requires preparation of the heart. To assist in this, each session suggests Bible passages for the team members to meditate on as they prepare for each meeting.

The theme

The programmes outlined here aim to help those with learning disabilities discover more about the person of God. Understanding what God is like is fundamental to faith. However, the intellectual limitations of people with learning disabilities require that this tremendous truth is presented on a level at which they can respond. As we have already noted, they have difficulty with abstract concepts. God has, however, anticipated this difficulty (which would affect us all but for divine initiative) and in at least two ways.

First, it is not a matter of theory alone – God revealed himself to us in his Son.

> In the past God spoke to our forefathers through the prophets at many times and in various ways, but in these last days he has spoken to us by his Son, whom he appointed heir of all things, and through whom he made the universe. *The Son is the radiance of God's glory and the exact representation of his being*, sustaining all things by his powerful word.
> *Hebrews 1:1–3, my italics*

> Philip said, 'Lord, show us the Father and that will be enough for us.
> Jesus answered: 'Don't you know me, Philip, even after I have been among you such a long time? *Anyone who has seen me has seen the Father.*'
> *John 14:8–9*

God says, 'Look at my Son. Believe in him.' And people with learning disabilities can certainly do that. Jesus taught his disciples that this was the principal way they could understand what God is like.

Second, this revelation shows that God is love. People with learning disabilities can certainly comprehend love, the basic ingredient of all good relationships. These sessions consider different aspects of God's love which Jesus' life proclaims so clearly. As we accompany him during his meetings with individuals and with enormous crowds, we witness repeatedly the depth of God's love in his Son. And, at the climax of these sessions, we consider the depth of God's love as we look at the arrest, trial and death of 'the Son of God, who loved me and gave himself for me' (Gal 2:20).

Session overview

Session 1: Introduction to the theme
Jesus shows us what God is like (John 14:8–9).

Session 2: God's love is kind
The healing of a little girl, Jairus' daughter (Mark 5:21–43). Jesus' command that she be given something to eat emphasises his kindness.

Session 3: God's love is strong
The story of the rich young man (Mark 10:17–22). 'Jesus looked at him and loved him': Jesus' love is so strong that he is able to love those who are not sure if they love him in return.

Session 4: God's love is great
The feeding of the five thousand (Mark 6:30–44). Jesus loved them and helped them: his love is so big that he wants to help large crowds of people.

Session 5: God's love is a caring love
The healing of blind Bartimaeus (Mark 10:46–52). Jesus asked Bartimaeus, 'What do you want me to do for you?' His love is a very caring love, and he listens to those who call out to him.

Session 6: God's love changes people
The story of Zacchaeus, the tax collector (Luke 19:1–10): Jesus came 'to seek and to save what was lost'. He loves people who are not very nice to know, and his love changes them.

Session 7: God's love is very wide
Jesus rides into Jerusalem (Mark 11:1–10; Luke 19:28–42). 'As he approached Jerusalem and saw the city, he wept over it': Jesus loved those who received him *and* those who rejected him. His love is very big.

Session 8: God wants us to remember his love
The Lord's supper (Luke 22:7–20). Jesus' words, 'Do this in remembrance of me', remind us of how much he loves us. He wants us to think about him.

Session 9: God's love is real
Jesus' arrest, trial and death (Luke 22 – 23; Mark 14 – 15). 'The Son of God, who loved me and gave himself for me' (Gal 2:20): Jesus did the biggest and best thing to show us that he loves us.

I hope you can already see how these profound truths can be made accessible for people with limited academic ability. Doesn't it excite you to think that our glorious God can be approached by *anyone* who has faith in his Son?

Session 1

Introduction to the theme

Aim
To show that we can understand what God is like by looking at Jesus, because he is God.

Objectives
- To arouse the interest of people with learning disabilities in knowing what God is like.
- To help them see that Jesus can show them what God is like.
- To encourage them to enjoy worship.

Preparation
YOU WILL NEED
- A map showing the Sea of Galilee and Bethsaida.
- Various attractive books, eg one on flowers or birds and one on cookery.
- A Bible.

PREPARING YOURSELF
Meditate on the following Bible passages:

- John 14:8–9.
- Hebrews 1:1–3.

PREPARING TO TEACH
This first session is built around what Jesus said to the disciples in the upper room (John 14:8–9). To lead into the theme, find a starting point which shows that we often learn things indirectly. The example used in the teaching sample shows how we can use books for this purpose. (Remember, the group may be more used to looking at books rather than reading them.) You may find that there are other ways to make the same point, but make sure that the point is obvious, that it can be explained simply and that it relates to the life experience of the group.

Develop the theme by explaining how the disciples were called, the years they spent with Jesus, and how he was teaching them what God is like. Take care to use words that people in your group understand, and avoid concepts they will not follow. (Note the way 'disciple' is introduced in the teaching sample below.) Think of ways to involve group members in the teaching. This session has a limited objective: prepare in such a way that it is achieved, and be content with that!

Teaching sample
When Jesus was here in our world, he called some people to follow him and to stay with him as his special friends. One day, when Jesus was out walking, he saw a man he wanted to speak to. So Jesus walked towards him. When he had come up to him, Jesus said, 'Follow me.' And the man did! The man's name was Philip. Philip lived in a little town near the Sea of Galilee, where lots of fishermen lived. The town was called Bethsaida.

(Use the map to show where Galilee and Bethsaida are.)

After Jesus said, 'Follow me' to Philip, Philip hurried along the road to find his friend, Nathanael. Philip wanted to tell Nathanael about Jesus. 'Come and meet Jesus,' Philip said to him. Nathanael did go and meet Jesus, and he became one of his special friends too.

Can you tell me what Jesus called his twelve special friends? Disciples. A disciple is a learner.

(An example of being 'a learner', which is appropriate to your group, may be helpful here.)

Jesus' twelve special friends, his disciples, spent a lot of time with him. Jesus wanted to teach them many things. What do you think Jesus wanted to tell his friends about? Who do you think Jesus wanted to tell his friends about? God.

The disciples were with Jesus when he healed people and made them really well again. They were with Jesus when he made the bad storm go away. And they heard Jesus talking to the crowds of people, telling them about God, his Father.

I think these twelve special friends of Jesus especially liked being with Jesus when the crowds of people had all gone home and only they were with him. Then they could be quiet and sometimes just chat to Jesus and ask him questions about God his Father. Jesus seemed very special to them.

The twelve disciples were with Jesus for three whole years, travelling with him wherever he went. I think they must have been very tired sometimes, don't you? Can you tell me the names of any of the disciples? Simon Peter, Andrew, James, John, Philip, Bartholomew, Thomas, Matthew, James the son of Alphaeus, Thaddaeus, Simon the Zealot and Judas Iscariot.

(Obviously, not everyone in your group will know these names, but some will be pleased to participate by giving you one or two.)

For how many years were these twelve men with Jesus? Not one, or two, but *three* years. And during that time Jesus talked to them a lot about God, his Father.

The night before Jesus died on the cross, he told his disciples that he was going back to heaven and in heaven he was going to get a special home ready for them. They could not understand what Jesus was saying. Then Philip said to Jesus, 'Lord, show us the Father and that will be enough for us.' Philip didn't understand what Jesus was saying about heaven, but he wanted to know what God is like. That's why he said, 'Show us the Father and that will be enough for us.' He was saying, 'We want to know God.'

What do you think God is like?

(Allow time for contributions, but do not be put off if no one responds. It is a big question!)

Jesus said to Philip, 'Anyone who has seen *me* has seen the Father.' Jesus was saying, 'I am God.'

We cannot see Jesus now as Philip did that day. But we can read and learn about Jesus in the Bible, so we can find out what God is like. Not everybody can read the Bible, but we can listen to someone talking about Jesus and telling us what the Bible says about him. This is what we are going to do together in this group.

Next time we meet together, we are going to learn about God being a loving person. Jesus shows us that God is love and he really cares a lot about us.

PREPARING FOR THE MEETING

Get the room ready in good time. The team should arrive early and all the necessary transport arrangements be worked out beforehand. Everyone involved should know what is expected of them! If possible, make every helper aware of the theme for the meeting.

Programme for the meeting

What follows is a suggested format for the very first meeting of the group.

WELCOME

It is important that those coming to the meeting are made to feel welcomed and valued. Spend time on introductions:

- Introduce the team members to everyone else.
- Introduce people in the group to one another (or in small groups).
- Introduce any (important) visitors, eg the minister/pastor/vicar.

Don't hurry this activity!

SONG

Explain that singing is a way of showing God that we think he is good. Jesus loves people to meet together to worship God. Jesus has promised to be with them when they do this.

Use a song which expresses this truth, for example 'As we are gathered, Jesus is here' (MP 38). Not all the words and concepts in this song will be understood, so just emphasise 'Jesus is here', which is repeated several times. Sing this song two or three times so that people can learn the words and understand that this time is special because we are meeting with Jesus.

Another possible choice is 'Come on and celebrate!' (MP 99). An explanation of some of the concepts in this song may be necessary.

PRAYER

Thank God for the good things he gives to us, especially friends and people who are kind to us. Thank him that we can meet him together. Thank him for his greatness ('bigness' might be better understood by the group). Thank God that he wants to be our friend. Ask him to help us know that he is meeting with us. Ask him to help us as we worship him and sing his praises.

SONGS

To create a greater appreciation of what God is like and what he does for us, use songs which convey the ideas you have talked about in the prayer time. Repetition will help people both to understand and remember. Possibilities include 'Thank You Jesus' (MP 633, verse 1 only) and 'This is the day' (MP 691).

Lead into the songs by asking who made the world. This may be too big and abstract a question for the group, so if necessary break it down into smaller questions: 'Who made the sky? Who made the trees? The flowers? The birds? The animals? Who made this day?'

Finally, lead into a song that is a response to God's greatness, beauty and love, eg the chorus only of 'God's love is great' (Causeway Music). 'Sing alleluia to the Lord' (MP 601) is a particularly simple song, and people who have not been able to sing previous songs may feel able to join in. Explain that 'alleluia' (or 'hallelujah') is a way of saying 'God is good'. Use as many verses as you feel is appropriate at this stage.

TEACHING 1

Introduce the person who will teach. It will be helpful if the teaching is in two parts, the first part an introduction followed by a break for singing, before moving on to the full 'lesson'.

The person teaching should display picture books in a way that everyone can see them. Ask the group which book we should look at if we wanted to find out something (perhaps a name or colour) about flowers or birds. Someone in the group is sure to make the right choice! Suggest that a friend, or an aunt or uncle, is coming to tea on Sunday. Which book should we look at to find out how to bake a cake? Which book should we look at to find out about God?

SONG

Teach the group 'Lord, You are more precious than silver' (MP 447), explaining what 'preciousness' means.

TEACHING 2

Follow up the introductory teaching as shown in the teaching sample.

REFLECTION AND PRAYER

Suggest a quiet period for people to think and pray. If it feels right, ask for one or two (not by name at this early stage of group) to thank God for something, eg the Bible, Jesus, his love, his care, something he has done.

SONGS

The songs you sing here are to help your group make some response to what they have been taught, eg 'The greatest thing in all my life' (MP 646). Talk about 'the greatest thing', the biggest thing, the best thing, so that you help people understand what they are singing about.

SHARING

By this time the group may be sufficiently relaxed for some to contribute. If this is the case, it would be good to ask if anyone in the group has something they would like to share with everyone, something they would like to talk about. You may get some surprising responses! Try to take what has been said and either add to it sensitively or perhaps link it to something you or others have already said during the meeting. It is important that people are made to feel their contributions are good.

Sharing may be slow to come, so be ready to cope with silence for a few moments – people may need time. This will become an increasingly worthwhile part of your meetings.

SONG

Ask the group if anyone would like to choose a song to end with, perhaps from those already sung. Have a suggestion ready in case no one wants to choose.

TAKE-HOME FOLDERS

If take-home papers and folders are being provided, explain what they are for and that everyone can have one. Don't impose these on people if they are reluctant to take one. Suggest parts that may be written over or coloured, if appropriate. If there is time, read the section which enforces the main point of the teaching session.

CONCLUSION

Close the meeting by thanking Jesus for being with you. Make sure everyone knows when the next meeting will be held – a printed list of dates would be helpful. Group members can keep these in their Bibles or folders. Also make sure that carers and those providing transport have a list of future meeting dates.

Evaluation and review

As this was the first meeting, there will probably be a number of improvements you want to make. Try to focus on three or four issues, asking the following questions:

Was the setting attractive?
Were people made to feel welcome?
Were they joining in the singing?
Was there any difficulty with the music?
Was the teacher listened to?
Could everybody hear what was being said?

As a team, reflect on how you could do better on these points next time round.

God's love is kind

Aim

To teach that God is love, emphasising his kindness.

Objectives

- To reinforce the understanding of people with learning disabilities that Jesus can show them what God is like.
- To show that God is interested in the ordinary aspects of our lives.
- To increase participation in the meeting.

Preparation

YOU WILL NEED

- Folders for any newcomers.
- A map showing the Sea of Galilee and Capernaum.
- Any props or equipment for sketches.

PREPARING YOURSELF

Spend some time meditating on passages that refer to God's kindness:

- 1 Samuel 20:1–17 (especially v14).
- Isaiah 54:7–10.
- Ephesians 2:1–10 (especially v7).
- Titus 3:3–7.

In your reflections on this theme, be clear about the distinction between love and kindness. Love is the emotion of which kindness is an expression.

PREPARING TO TEACH

The introduction

To lead into the teaching time, members of the team could act out two sketches illustrating love that is expressed in kindness. The sketches may need to be drafted by the person doing the teaching, to ensure that they introduce the teaching adequately. As you compose them, keep in mind the settings familiar to people with learning disabilities.

Sketch 1

One person show kindness towards another who is sad – perhaps because she is worried about a sick parent or relative.

Sketch 2

Someone shows kindness to another by offering to help with the washing up, rather than leaving it all to him while everyone else enjoys the party.

(In due course people with learning disabilities will be able to take part in the sketches.)

Those taking part should try to use notes rather than read from a script. If reading is unavoidable, eye contact should be maintained as much as possible.

The subject

Read the Gospel accounts of the healing of Jairus' daughter (Matt 9:18–26; Mark 5:21–43; Luke 8:40–56). You will notice that two stories are interwoven, both clearly showing Jesus' kindness. Be careful to keep your focus primarily on the healing of the little girl, but let the healing of the woman enhance facets of Jesus' kindness.

Prepare a retelling of the narrative, again taking care to use simple language. Endeavour to tell the story in a vivid and lively manner – the events must have been dramatic. Imagine the embarrassed hush when Jesus asked who touched him; the frustration Jairus must have felt at the delay; his sadness at seeing his daughter dead. Try to involve the group in some way, for example ask them to suggest names for Jairus' wife and daughter. (Nudge them towards Jewish names!)

The application is very important. There are two issues to think through:

- How people with learning disabilities may experience God's kindness towards them.
- How they in turn can show love by being kind to other people.

Teaching sample

The last time we met together I said that we were going to learn about God being a loving person. Jesus said, 'Anyone who has seen me has seen the Father.' Jesus shows us that God is love and cares a lot about us. How do we know that someone loves us?

(By the things they say and do – bring out a response here.)

Today we are going to talk about a family who lived in a town called Capernaum, near the Sea of Galilee, where Jesus spent a lot of his time while he was here in our world.

(Use the map to show the location of the Sea of Galilee and Capernaum.)

In this family there was a father and a mother and a little girl who was 12 years old. The father's name was Jairus. The Bible doesn't tell us the names of the mother or the little girl. Would someone like to choose a name for the little girl?

(Have one ready yourself in case there is no response. Ask them to suggest a name for the mother too. They could be biblical names; suggest this if some of your group are familiar with Bible.)

Jairus was an important man in Capernaum. You see, there was a large synagogue there. Does anyone know what a synagogue is?

(The place where the Jews meet for worship; also the place for prayer and for teachers to study.)

Every synagogue had a man who was in charge, who was called a 'ruler'. If it was a big synagogue, it would have two or three rulers. The rulers in the synagogues took the services and told other people to take part in the services. Special visitors were asked to read sometimes (see Mark 1:21–22). Jesus had talked in the service at the Capernaum synagogue. I wonder if Jairus was leading the service on the day that Jesus spoke? He might have been. Perhaps he realised then that Jesus was special and different from other people who spoke in the synagogue. Because Jairus had an important job, I expect he was probably quite rich and lived in a very nice house with his wife and his daughter.

Jesus had been away from Capernaum. He had been very busy speaking to people and healing those who were unwell. He got into a boat and went across the Sea of Galilee to Capernaum. While Jesus was in the boat, he could have a rest and talk to his Father in heaven. As soon as he got out of the boat, a crowd of people came to him. They wanted to hear Jesus speak, and perhaps they wanted to see him heal somebody.

Jairus must have heard that Jesus was coming to his town. He was feeling very worried and thought Jesus might be willing to help him. His daughter had become ill, and every day she was getting weaker.

(Use the name chosen for her by the group.)

Jairus knew that Jesus had helped other sick people to become well again, and wondered if Jesus would come to his house to see his daughter. He decided to ask Jesus to do this.

Jairus told his wife what he wanted to do and said goodbye to her. Then he joined the crowds of people who were already out in the streets because they too had heard that Jesus was in their town. The people walking in front of Jairus slowed him down, and he had to push his way through them until he came to Jesus. Jairus knew that Jesus was a special person sent by God, and he fell down on his knees in front of him. Looking up into Jesus' face, he said, 'My daughter is dying. Please come and put your hand on her so that she will be healed and live.'

Jairus was shaking as he waited to hear what Jesus would say. He thought of his daughter lying on her bed at home, looking so unwell. He didn't want her to die. He loved her very much. 'I will come with you and see your daughter,' said Jesus. How relieved Jairus felt! Now he could really begin to hope that his daughter would get well again! Jesus went with Jairus straightaway, and all the crowds of people followed them. But on the way something unexpected happened.

There was a lady in the crowd who was very ill. No doctor had been able to make her better. She thought that if she just touched the edge of Jesus' long coat she would get better. She pushed her way gently through the crowds of people, and reached out her hand to touch Jesus' coat. As soon as she touched it, she became well. None of the crowd took any notice of the lady, but Jesus did. He knew she had wanted him to heal her. Jesus stood still and said, 'Who touched me?' The lady was very shy, but slowly she walked towards Jesus and told him that she had touched him.

Jairus was getting very worried about Jesus stopping to talk to the lady like this. He knew that his little girl was very ill and if Jesus didn't get to her soon she would die. While Jesus was still talking to the lady, one of Jairus' friends came to look for him. When he found him he said, 'Your daughter is dead. Why bother the teacher (Jesus) any more?' Jesus heard him say this. He turned to Jairus and said, 'Don't be afraid. Just believe.' Jesus knew that Jairus was worried and upset, and he wanted to help him feel better. How kind Jesus is.

They walked on quickly towards Jairus' home. Jesus took three of his special friends, disciples, into the house with him. Their names were Peter, James and John. When they walked through the door into the house, they heard a lot of noise. People were crying very loudly. Jesus said to the people, 'Why all this noise and crying? The child is not dead but asleep.' And the people laughed at him. Jesus sent them all outside. He wanted to be quiet. Jesus took Jairus, his wife *(use the names the group has suggested)*, Peter, James and John with him into the room where the girl lay dead. Jesus went over to her, took hold of her hand and said to her: '*Talitha koum*'.

Why did Jesus say, '*Talitha koum*'? They sound like funny words to us, don't they? But they were not funny or strange to Jairus or his wife or their daughter. They were the words that her mother and father would have used when they woke her up in the morning. '*Talitha koum*' means 'Little girl, I say to you, get up!' She had been dead, but straightaway when Jesus spoke she opened her eyes. I expect the first thing she saw was Jesus' lovely face. Then she saw her mother and father looking down at her. She got up and walked around the room. Jairus and his wife, Peter, James and John were amazed! They had never seen a dead person come back to life before! It seemed as if she had just been sleeping and then woken up fresh and well.

Jesus is a very special person, isn't he? He is the Son of God. Only God can make people come alive again. Jairus and his wife could hardly believe their eyes as they watched their daughter walk around the room and then run towards them! She had been so ill! She had died! But now, because Jesus touched her and talked to her, she was well again. Jesus looked at Jairus and said, 'Do not let anyone know about this'.

Jesus had done something very special for the girl. He said to her mother, 'Give her something to eat.' How kind Jesus is!

We said earlier that we know if someone loves us by what they say to us and what they do for us. Jesus loves everyone. I'm sure that when Jairus' little girl opened her eyes and saw Jesus' face, she knew that Jesus loved her. She may not have seen him before, but she was not afraid of him. She could tell straightaway that he loved her. Jesus spoke kind words to her. He held her hand gently. He told her parents to give her something to eat. Jesus knew what she needed. He cared a lot about her.

Jesus showed Jairus and his family what God, his Father, is like – a loving person. Yes, God is love.

Jesus is with his Father God in heaven now. He still loves everyone – that means you and me, everyone here! He loves each one of us the same. Isn't that good? Jesus likes to tell us and show us that he loves us. Do you remember how kind Jesus was to Jairus when he was worried about his little girl? 'Don't be afraid. Just trust me,' Jesus said to him. Jairus did trust Jesus and Jesus brought his little girl back to life. All the family were happy again. Jesus was kind to *(the little girl's name)*'s mother too. She had been so sad because her lovely daughter was so ill and died. And Jesus was kind to *(the little girl's name)*. Jesus gave her life. He knew what she needed – something to eat and something to drink – and he told her parents to give this to her.

It is good to know that Jesus is still kind. He will be kind to us. He knows when we are ill, and he wants us to feel better. To know that someone cares about us really helps us when we are ill. God cares about us all the time and still provides what we need. We need good food and drink. We need sleep. We need friends. We need somewhere to live. God knows all about these thing, and he gives us what we need. God is kind to us because he loves us.

PREPARING FOR THE MEETING
Arrange to make any changes to the meeting room which have been agreed on by the team following the previous session.

Does more thought need to be given to welcoming people? If the people with learning disabilities who come are strangers to each other, make sure that helpers chat with them on arrival and introduce them to one another.

Team members should glean any news from people as they arrive, and inform the leader of anything significant. The person who leads the time of sharing may then use this to draw individuals into making a contribution later in the meeting. Ensure that anyone who might be worried or upset about something has support.

Programme for the meeting
WELCOME
Introduce the team members again. Take particular notice of any newcomers, and make sure everyone knows their names.

PRAYER
Lead in prayer briefly, to help people settle and to increase their awareness that God is in the room with them.

SONGS
As this is only the second meeting and people may need reassurance, it will help to begin with a song from the previous meeting, eg 'Come on and celebrate!' (MP 99), or, if one song used last time went really well, use that again. Sing it through twice to establish familiarity. Then sing the chorus only of 'God's love is great' (CM). Teach the group one new song, eg 'Hosanna, hosanna, hosanna in the highest' (MP 242, explain that 'Hosanna!' means 'Save now!').

SHARING
Invite people to share news of recent events or personal matters they would like the group to pray for. Use information gleaned earlier to encourage bashful people to participate, but don't put them under pressure.

This would be a good point at which to have someone read out a few verses from a psalm. By now the readers in the group may have been identified, and could be asked beforehand if they would like to read. They may not!

INTRODUCTION TO TEACHING
Use the two sketches (p 35) to set the scene for the teaching session.

SONG
Sing 'Open our eyes, Lord' (MP 545). Do not go into a long and detailed explanation of the concepts in this song. Simply explain that these words are a prayer to God, asking him to help us to feel close to him and to listen to him in the teaching session.

TEACHING
Use the two sketches as your way in, introducing the theme that kindness is something that starts with God.

REFLECTION AND PRAYER
It might be appropriate to break into small groups at this point, if this can be done relatively easily without distracting from the teaching, in order to give people time to consider quietly what has been said and to respond. Team members should take responsibility for leading the groups.

Some may want to pray aloud, others may enjoy the quiet. Pray that the Holy Spirit will help people understand what has been taught. Team members can remind those in their groups of how kind Jesus was to Jairus and his family, how he showed them that God is love. Talk about God being kind to us.

Suggest that group members thank Jesus for showing us that God loves us. It may be appropriate to ask some of them if they have anything in particular to thank God for. Suggest that they ask Jesus to help them be loving and kind, and do kind things for others. If possible, talk about individuals who need help, and assist people in the group to see how they can help. Pray about this together.

(It may be better now to stay in the small groups until the end of the meeting.)

SONGS
The song 'Jesus raised the one they thought was dead' may be sung, or a taped recording of it played (available from Causeway Music).

Assess whether or not it would be more helpful to sing a familiar song. Choose sensitively so that the evening is brought to an appropriate conclusion. Suggestions are 'When I feel the touch' (MP 753), 'Thank You Jesus' (MP 633, verses 1 and 2), and 'God is good' (MP 185).

TAKE-HOME PAPERS
Refer to some aspect of the paper which reinforces your teaching. Encourage group members to bring their folders to each meeting and to show others any writing or colouring they have done.

CONCLUSION
Teach the group to say the benediction to each other: 'The grace of the Lord Jesus Christ be with us all'. Make sure that everyone knows the date of the next meeting. Make a mental note of any who came to the first meeting but not to this one.

Evaluation and review
There may still be problems with the venue. Identify what these are and how to resolve them before the next meeting. Iron out any problems with transport. Discuss whether the group's participation was successful. Try to identify the things that worked well.

- What were the most helpful contributions?
- If someone said too much, how should that be dealt with in future?
- Did people join in prayer in the small groups?

Share the list of absentees for prayer and informal follow-up.

Session 3

God's love is strong

Aim
To emphasise the strength of God's love.

Objectives
- To create awareness of a spiritual dimension to life by introducing the possibility of knowing God.
- To help people with learning disabilities realise that they must respond to God's love and its demands.
- To show that being good is not sufficient in itself to create a relationship with God.

Preparation
By now you will know the people attending the group and their level of ability. The meeting should now be geared towards matching their particular needs. The material provided for this and subsequent sessions assumes that progressively less assistance will be required.

YOU WILL NEED
- A map showing the journey from Capernaum to Judea.

PREPARING YOURSELF
God's love is strong in that it is not weakened by a feeble response to him on our part. Reflect on some examples of this divine passion in scripture:

- Deuteronomy 4:25–31.
- Hosea 11.
- Luke 15:11–32.
- John 17.

PREPARING TO TEACH
Start by reading the Gospel accounts of the rich young man's meeting with Jesus (Matt 19:16–22; Mark 10:17–22; Luke 18:18–23).

The teaching can be done in two parts. The first part is a retelling of the narrative, followed by a mime of the incident. The account is quite short, consisting only of a conversation between Jesus and a rich young man, in the region of Judea. To make the 'story' interesting, try to imagine the scene yourself and to convey the liveliness of this as you tell of the encounter: this will help the mime that follows. Be careful how you use words so that you are clearly understood. Note how brave this young man was: he came and knelt down before Jesus in front of the inevitable crowd of people gathered around him. His desire to receive eternal life must have been strong. But he was not prepared to pay the cost, to make God first in his affections.

Team members should be ready to lead the mime of the story. Two actors, both of whom can be people with learning disabilities, will be needed – one to act the part of Jesus and the other the part of the rich young man. They should be asked whether they want to participate, and prepared, before the meeting begins. The most important part of the mime will be the expressions on the faces of the young man and Jesus, particularly at the end when the young man walks away looking sad and Jesus watches him go, also looking sad. Everyone else can be the crowd.

The second part of the teaching develops the story and the application. This will be the main part of the teaching, and it will require careful preparation. The group may have only the vaguest idea of the spiritual dimension to their lives. They may know the phrase 'eternal life' but be quite unaware of its meaning or of its importance for them. In the teaching sample, note that eternal life is 'translated' as 'being with God here and in heaven'.

Teaching sample (second part)
When Jesus looked at the rich young man, he saw a good man who had kept most of God's commandments – perhaps all of them except the first. Jesus saw that the man loved his money more than he loved God. The man's attitude to his money and possessions had to change if he was to receive eternal life.

'There's one thing wrong with you,' Jesus said to the young man. 'If you want to have life with God, you must go and sell everything you have and give your money to help poor people. After that, you can enjoy life with God here and in heaven. Then come and follow me.'

When the young man heard Jesus say, 'Sell everything you have', he was very sad. His face showed how unhappy he felt. He loved his money and all the lovely things he had bought with it. He didn't want to give them away. Jesus had said he must do this before he could really please God. His love for his money and things filled his heart. There was no room for Jesus in his heart.

Still looking very sad, the young man got up and walked away from Jesus. But as Jesus saw him walking away, he still felt strong love in his heart for the young man.

Jesus isn't like us. We like some people, but there are other people we do not like, especially those who are unkind to us. We find it hard to like them and to feel love in our hearts for them. Because Jesus is God's Son, his love for people never changes. He really does love us all the time, even when we don't love him very much. If we thank Jesus for loving us and ask him to take away the bad things we have said or thought about or done, we will then be able to feel and know his love always! Even on those days when we think we have not loved him as much as we want to, we can still be sure that he loves us and that he wants us to feel safe and loved.

Remember how Jesus looked at that rich young man who walked away from him: he 'looked at him and loved him'. Jesus looks at us and loves us. He is the best friend we can ever have! We can be sure of his love.

What is in our hearts? What do we love best? We need to think about that. Jesus wants us to love him first. He wants us to love other people, too. God has loved us with all his heart. How do we know that? Because he gave us the Lord Jesus, his dear Son, whom he loved very much. He gave him to die for us, so that the bad things we have done can be taken away and we can feel his love. Jesus looks at you and loves you. Will you love him with all your heart?

PREPARING FOR THE MEETING

Make the improvements that the team agreed together when you reviewed the last meeting – people may have to be organised to do this. Check that absentees from the last meeting have been followed up. Arrange the seating so as to allow enough space for the mime.

Keep on introducing people to one another and helping them get to know each other's names. At the last meeting group members were encouraged to bring in any colouring or work they had done on the take-home papers, and the team could facilitate this now.

After the session, some of the group may want to make a response and not know what to do. Encourage the team to talk with people afterwards so as to follow up this need to respond to God's love. Warn them, though, against any pressurising!

Programme for the meeting

SONGS

By now there will be some firm favourites which the group sings well. If these are fairly lively, the meeting will get off to a good start. Have joyful songs early on, then make the meeting more reflective as it proceeds. Include familiar songs, such as 'This is the day' (MP 691) or 'Jesus, Name above all names' (MP 375).

There should be at least one other worship session during the meeting, perhaps after the teaching. Songs that encourage faith would be helpful here, eg 'Believe on the Lord Jesus', and you could introduce the group to 'The Father himself loves you' (both Causeway Music). Other possibilities are 'We are here to praise You' (MP 717) and 'We will praise the name of Jesus' (CM).

PRAYER

Help people to be aware that they need to respond to God. The fact that he is someone we can know could be the focus for praise, leading to prayer that each person present will come to know him. Encourage people to share any concerns that they want prayer for.

SHARING

You might consider having this at another point in the meeting. It may be a useful means of getting the meeting under way while ensuring that latecomers do not miss the worship and teaching.

TEACHING 1

Tell the story as vividly and realistically as possible, helping people to 'feel' the scene and to catch its sadness.

MIME AND READING

Group members can now participate in acting out the story. Give a few instructions, so that people are happy about taking part. Accompany the mime by reading the incident in Mark's account, which emphasises Jesus' love. Pace the readings so as to give time for the 'actors' to play their parts to the full. Tell everyone to sit down when the mime is finished.

TEACHING 2

Refer back to the story as told and mimed. Relate what has been seen and heard to the people in the group by picking up the important theme and applying it to them. Explain that because he is God's Son, Jesus can see us as we really are: he knows what we think; he knows what we love.

REFLECTION AND PRAYER

Encourage people to think about what they really love best. Remind them that Jesus' love is strong, that he will never stop loving them. Suggest that everyone thinks about how important it is to love Jesus first.

Evaluation and review

Every group will have its extroverts – those who grab all the attention by their exuberance, chattiness and warmth. They are a tremendous asset! But check how the team are relating to the quiet, shy people, those who speak with difficulty if at all. Ask yourselves:

- Did people understand what was being said?
- Was there more participation this time?
- Was there any evidence that people wanted to respond to God's love? Should this be followed up in any way? By whom?

God's love is great

Aim

To show that God's love is big enough to include everyone.

Objectives

- To show that God's heart is moved by the needs of groups or crowds of people.
- To help people with learning disabilities to realise that God cares about every part of their lives, both physical and spiritual.
- To show that our love for others will make us want to help them.

Preparation

YOU WILL NEED
- A map showing the region of Galilee.

PREPARING YOURSELF

In the previous session the focus was on God's love for the individual. This time the focus shifts to show that no one is overlooked – God cares for everyone.

Remind yourself of God's universal interest in people by reflecting on the following:

- Matthew 15:32–36.
- Matthew 28:16–20.
- Mark 1:35–39.
- Luke 18:15–17.
- John 4:34–42.
- Acts 1:8.
- Romans 15:17–21.

PREPARING TO TEACH.

Start by reading thoroughly the Gospel accounts of the feeding of the five thousand (Matt 14:13–21; Mark 6:30–44; Luke 9:10–17; John 6:1–15).

These accounts are rich in detail and contain many gems of truth. The more they are read and reflected on, the more lively and real the retelling will be. Mark relates happenings leading up to this event, and each of the other Gospel writers adds a distinctive detail. Make a list of these, for example:

> The number of those who ate was about 5,000 men, besides women and children.
>
> *Matthew 14:21*

> He welcomed them and spoke to them about the kingdom of God, and healed those who needed healing.
>
> *Luke 9:11*

> Then Jesus went up a mountainside and sat down with his disciples…

> When Jesus looked up and saw a great crowd coming towards him, he said to Philip, 'Where shall we buy bread for these people to eat?'…
>
> Philip answered him, 'Eight months' wages would not buy enough bread for each one to have a bite!'
>
> Another of his disciples, Andrew, Simon Peter's brother, spoke up, 'Here is a boy with five small barley loaves and two small fish, but how far will they go among so many?'
>
> *John 6:3–9*

Decide how to retell the story – presenting the account as an eye-witness would be very effective. Here are some other possibilities:

- Tell the story as though you were one of the crowd, who so wanted to hear what Jesus was teaching about his Father, God, that you walked almost all round the shore of the lake to hear him.
- Get 'inside' Philip or Andrew, and speak as though they were telling an old friend what took place.
- Become the boy whose lunch Jesus used to miraculously create enough to feed the huge crowd.

Think about how to convey an impression of the scale of what took place. The size of the crowd is greater than the number of people we are used to seeing together at one time. People with learning disabilities will have little concept of how large it was, and will need help. Those who have been to Spring Harvest may remember that the Big Top holds about 5,000 people. Alternatively, show slides of crowd scenes, or make a video recording of newscasts of crowds and play it back. Suitable posters would achieve the same end.

The aim, remember, is to show that God loves everyone, so be sure to draw out from the story that God's love was big enough for this huge crowd. Show how it was expressed:

> When Jesus landed and saw a large crowd, he had compassion on them, because they were like sheep without a shepherd. So he began teaching them many things.
>
> *Mark 6:34*

Note too that 'he welcomed them' (Luke 9:11). Notice how Jesus' heart was moved deeply, and he had to do something immediately to meet the spiritual needs of these people. He saw them as having no direction in their lives, and responded to that by speaking to them about his Father. The disciples were aware of the physical needs of this enormous crowd and wanted to send them away, thus removing any sense of responsibility they may have had to do something; but Jesus told them, 'They do not need to go away. You give them something to eat.' Although what the disciples had was so small and inadequate, it was important that Jesus received it from them before providing for the needs of the crowd.

PREPARING FOR THE MEETING

This session is about a picnic. If the weather is warm and fine, why not turn it into an evening picnic? The whole meeting then becomes a teaching aid! But choose your location carefully lest there are so many distractions that no one listens to the teaching. A large garden would be a suitable place. Consider enlisting more helpers for the evening.

Prepare a sample meal comparable in quantity with the five loaves (or barley cakes about the size of a bread roll) and two fish (cheese might be less messy).

Set up slides or a video in advance so that they can be shown with the minimum of disruption and distraction. Make sure the video does not overrun on to other pre-recorded material.

If the eye-witness approach is used, the speaker should put on something suitable for the part when she begins to play her role. She should tell people what her costume means, take it off before going on to make the teaching application, and afterwards show that she is herself again. Otherwise group members may be worrying where Sarah (or whoever) has gone!

Teaching sample

What follows is the application: see above and the meeting programme for other elements.

When we look at crowds of people, we may feel that there are too many for us to help them. Sometimes we see films on television that show crowds of very poor people who do not have enough to eat. We feel sorry that they are hungry and ill, but we do not know how we can help them.

As Jesus looked at the big crowd of people, who had followed him by running and walking around the lakeside until they found him, he really felt sorry for them. However, there were not too many people for him to help. Jesus thought, 'These people need someone to tell them how God wants them to live. I must tell them about my Father and his love for them.' And you will remember that this is what he did.

But when he had finished talking, the people didn't go away. They stayed on the hillside with Jesus and his disciples, where they had been all day without any food. Do you remember where the food came from to feed this big crowd? One boy's lunch had to feed thousands of people! Jesus didn't just love a few people in the crowd: he loved them all, and wanted to help them all. He wanted to show them that God's love is very big, very great. God knows it is important that we feel loved. God gives us friends and family to love us and care about us. He gave us Jesus to come and live in our world, and to show us what God is like. God is love, and his love is great!

God likes to show us that he loves us. He wants to show us how to live happy lives and to know that we are important to him. Do you think you are important to God? You are important to him, because he made you and because he gave Jesus to die for you. His love is very big, very great. It was hard for Jesus to die for us, but he wanted to do it

because he loves us so much and wants to take from us all the bad things we have done. Jesus wants to help us live as happy people who are sure that God loves us. He will give us everything we need.

When we really understand how much God loves us, we will want to love other people. We will want to help them when they need something. Jesus broke the bread and the fish, and gave it to his disciples, and they gave it to the people. Jesus wants us to work with him to show people that God loves them very much and wants to help them. We don't need to be clever, or strong, or rich to help people. Jesus can help us to help them.

Think of one person you can help this week. You may like to come and talk to me before you go home today, and tell me who you are going to help. Then I will ask God to help you do it.

Programme for the meeting

SETTING THE ATMOSPHERE

The crowd following Jesus may have been in high spirits. Lots of people were healed, and they and their friends would have been very excited and happy. A similar atmosphere of joy can be established in the group through your choice of songs and in the prayer time.

SONGS

Expand your repertoire further. Here are some that fit this session: 'Be still and know that I am God' (MP 48), 'The Father himself loves you' (CM), 'Open our eyes, Lord' (MP 545), 'When I feel the touch' (MP 753), 'God is good – we sing and shout it' (MP 185), 'God's love is great' (CM).

Look through the words of these songs to see whether any explanation is required. Give people time to learn new ones. Remember, they may not be able to read the words.

PARTICIPATION

More people in the group should feel able to participate in a greater number of ways. Sharing news, concerns and matters for prayer, as well as Bible reading, can be enriched as more people are involved. Remember to ask someone to pray for the person who will be giving the teaching session.

TEACHING

You may find it desirable to have this in two parts separated by one or two songs. In the first part, discuss together how to plan a picnic, encouraging as much participation as possible. Help people to think about packing their own lunch, and talk about how much each person would need. Use the meal you have already prepared. Then show slides or the video to help the group understand how many people attended Jesus' picnic. Talk about how far your lunch would feed them! Refer back to the visuals you used to help people understand the vastness of the crowd who came to Jesus.

The second part consists of retelling the story as an eye-witness account, followed by the application outlined in the teaching sample.

REFLECTION AND PRAYER

It may be appropriate for team members to follow up the emphasis on helping others. If they make a note of who wants to do what, they will be able to ask how individual group members got on at the next meeting.

In closing, encourage the group to remember that God loves them wherever they will be during the next week or two.

Evaluation and review

Four sessions have now been completed. The team should be feeling a stronger sense of their own identity as a group. The practical problems about, say, the venue, the transport or the overhead projector are probably resolved.

It would be sensible at this stage to evaluate the strengths of the team so that people are using their gifts and abilities well. If one person is better at retelling narratives and another strong on relevant application, be prepared to rearrange the teaching so as to build on those strengths. Talk honestly about how the meetings are led. Is there one team member whose real strength is helping people with learning disabilities to participate? Encourage them to use that strength. Don't expect people with learning disabilities to put up with second-best because the team can't be honest in helping each other. Remember who the meetings are supposed to benefit!

Session 5

God's love is a caring love

Aim

To show that God's love is an actively caring love.

Objectives

- To show that God cares about people in need.
- To show that God listens to people who ask him for help.
- To help people with learning disabilities to understand that God will help them if they ask him.

Preparation

YOU WILL NEED

- A map showing Jericho.

PREPARING YOURSELF.

Consider how God cares for people who suffer rejection. Reflect on how this is expressed in the following verses:

- Genesis 21:1–21.
- Psalms 52, 54, 56, 57, 59.
- Psalm 69:6–18.

PREPARING TO TEACH.

Make yourself thoroughly familiar with the Gospel accounts of the story of Bartimaeus (Matt 20:29–34; Mark 10:46–52; Luke 18:35–43).

Try to understand what life was like for Bartimaeus so that you will be better able to help the group understand the events of the story. His experience and theirs have several common features which can be summed up in one word – rejection. Read the narratives and note in particular the attitudes shown by the crowd towards Bartimaeus. Then reflect on the attitudes that are frequently shown towards people with learning disabilities.

People with learning disabilities sense immediately whether they are loved and valued by the way they are looked at, spoken to and welcomed … the negative self-image they have of themselves comes from the image others have of them.

Jean Vanier, founder of L'Arche

The results of a life-time of rejection cannot be changed in one evening, but a sense of dignity and worth can begin to be rebuilt in people for whom this may be quite new. However, they will not be convinced that they are valued by God if they are not valued by the people around them. Ask God to help each person on the team see members of the group as he sees them.

Role-play is an effective way of conveying the wonder of this event. Telling the story as Bartimaeus can express the wonder and excitement of what happened.

As a preliminary to the teaching (or as part of it), it is imperative that people understand what blindness is and how much it disables a person. Inviting individuals to wear a blindfold while doing a simple task may achieve this. However, some will be frightened by being unable to see, so proceed with caution!

This time the teaching sample leaves the application for the speaker to prepare. Try to understand what it is like to experience rejection: people are stared at, laughed at or spoken to as if they were children. Emphasise how Jesus values us for ourselves, not for what we can do or how beautiful we are.

Teaching sample

A monologue – Bartimaeus is speaking:

It is a lovely sunny day again here in Jericho, and I am just going to work. You may not think this is very special, but it is for me. You see, until a few months ago I was a beggar.

Every day friends of mine took hold of my arms and led me along the road just outside the city of Jericho. They sat me down on the side of the road, and went off to do their day's work. I could not go to work in those days. Nobody wanted me to work for them. They thought I was useless because I was blind. I just sat by the side of the road, day after day, with the dust blowing up into my face as people hurried by. I must have looked quite a sight. Most people wished I wasn't there.

When you are blind, you use your ears a lot. Does that sound funny? Well, what I mean is, because you can't see things you listen extra hard to try to find out what is happening around you. Jericho is quite a busy town, and all day long people walked by me as they went to the shops or visited friends. I could hear the noise of their sandals on the stony road and the chatter of their voices as they talked to each other. Sometimes I heard little children running and laughing. It was always good to hear those sounds. I would call out to people as they walked by, and ask them for a little money. I didn't want a lot, just a little to buy myself enough food each day. I was very poor because I could not work. I didn't really want to be rich, but I did need food like everyone else. The only way I could buy food was to beg from people who walked past.

In the middle of the day, at dinner time, it became quieter along the road because the sun shining overhead was very hot. Most people went into their houses or sat under trees to be in the shade and not have the sun shining down on them. I had to stay where my friends had put me, and sometimes I got a headache because the sun was so hot.

One day, after my friends had sat me down at the side of the road, I heard a lot of noise. As I listened to the sounds, I realised that there must be a large crowd of people coming along the road towards the city of Jericho. Yes, as they got nearer to me I could hear the buzz of lots of people chatting to each other, and I could hear the sound of sandals on the dusty, stony road. The noise got louder and louder. There must be an enormous crowd of people coming, I thought to myself. Whatever is happening?

'Hey, someone, please tell me what is happening,' I called out. 'Jesus of Nazareth is coming,' someone shouted back at me.

Jesus! Coming along this road! Jesus, the Son of God! I've heard a lot about him. I have heard how he has helped and healed many people. I thought that he must be the special person God had been promising to send us. He was coming along my road! I must speak to him.

So I began to call out as loudly as I could: 'Jesus! Jesus! Son of David! Have mercy on me. Jesus! Jesus!'

Some people in the crowd got angry with me and told me to be quiet. It was always like this. As long as I can remember, people pushed me around, told me to be quiet and treated me as though I was useless. But I wanted Jesus to hear me, so I shouted louder: 'Jesus! Son of David! Have mercy on me!'

Some people came and took hold of my arms, saying, 'Cheer up! On your feet! Jesus is calling *you*!' I held onto them as they helped me up. I was shaking with excitement. Jesus had heard me and was now calling for *me*! The people led me to Jesus.

Then I had the most wonderful moment in my life. I heard Jesus' voice for the first time, and he was speaking just to me.

'What do you want me to do for you?' he asked.

I didn't have to think for long to answer his question. 'Lord, I want to see,' I said. I was still trembling with excitement!

Then I heard his voice again: 'Receive your sight; your faith has healed you.' And, at that moment, the miracle happened – I could see!!

Do you know what I saw first? Jesus' face, looking at me! It was wonderful. His eyes were so bright, and I knew he loved me. I felt at that moment that I just wanted to stay there, looking at his face for ever! It was so beautiful, so kind.

Looking at Jesus seemed to do something to me deep inside. It filled me with a deep love for God, and I began to speak out my praises to him. Then other people in the crowd, who had seen Jesus heal me, joined in. We praised God together. There was such joy in their faces as they shouted out praise to God. Now I could see their faces too, because Jesus had touched me and healed me.

What a day that was! I will never forget it. My life has been different ever since I heard his voice and felt his love and power working in my body. It is different because now I can see. It is different because now I can work. What a beautiful world God has made for us to enjoy. I like to watch the leaves on the trees moving very gently when there is a light wind. I like to see children playing happily together. I like to remember the joy in people's faces as they saw Jesus heal me. Their hearts were so full of praise to God, and so is mine.

Jesus is the Son of God, the special person God promised to send us. There is no one else like him. And he loves you as much as he loves me. You may not be blind as I was, but perhaps you need him to help you in other ways. Do you remember what he said to me when I stood in front of him? 'What do you want me to do for you?' I think he is saying that to you today. Jesus says, 'What do you want me to do for you?' You can tell him what you need, and he will listen to you.

(Now tell the group that you are no longer Bartimaeus. Make your application of the teaching as relevant as possible.)

Programme for the meeting
SONGS
Use some familiar songs, then extend the repertoire of the group by teaching them some new ones. Possible songs include 'Lord, You are so precious to me' (SOF 369), 'Jesus has given me' (an echo song) and 'The joy of the Lord' (both Causeway Music). You could also add verses 1–3 to 'Jesus, how lovely You are!' (MP 361).

TEACHING
Using the map, try to convey something of the atmosphere of old Jericho, which is situated in the hot Jordan valley. There may be an activity you could do together, to help get across an understanding of blindness.

REFLECTION AND PRAYER
If possible, split into small groups of not more than four. Helpers should encourage people to talk about their needs and what they want Jesus to do for them. Then spend time helping them to express these to Jesus in prayer.

People with no Christian background may need to be taught how to pray and what may be appropriately prayed about. Someone who is praying for characters in television soap operas is probably saying, 'I don't know how to pray.' They need to understand that God wants them to talk to him about the real concerns of people they know personally. They also need help in understanding that God is really interested in us and what concerns us. If there are only one or two people for whom this is a problem, put them together in a small group where they can receive help at each meeting.

Evaluation and review

Are group members getting to know one another? Do they welcome each other, talk to each other, call one another by name? Would it be helpful to arrange some social function which could encourage progress in this respect?

Has the meeting been visited by church leaders? If the group is connected to a particular church, the minister and church officers should have visited the meeting by now. Maybe they are waiting for an invitation! If the group is from more than one church, invite the church leaders to visit in turn.

Session 6

God's love changes people

Aim

To show that God's love changes people from being self-centred to caring about others.

Objectives

- To show that no one is too bad to be loved by God.
- To show that Jesus knows what is in our hearts.
- To help people with learning disabilities to understand that God's love can change them.

Preparation

YOU WILL NEED

- A map showing Jericho.

PREPARING YOURSELF

What a good thing it is that God takes the initiative in changing us. Spend some time reflecting on:

- Luke 15:1–7.
- John 10:1–18.
- Romans 5:1–11.
- 2 Corinthians 3:18.

PREPARING TO TEACH

Read Luke 19:1–10 carefully and thoughtfully. The account is very positive about Zacchaeus, so be sure to represent that in telling the story. Two options are suggested:

- *A monologue.* This could be read aloud, but would benefit by seeming to be a spontaneous description of events as they unfold.
- *A dramatic and imaginary presentation.* Try to persuade some members of the church who don't attend the group to perform this 'playlet'. In this way, you will increase the number of people who have some involvement in the group. While it is not essential that they follow the script exactly, the actors should be aware of the limited vocabulary of group members.

The application provided below can be adapted to suit either of these options. Think carefully about the group so as to make the application fit issues they face. Show that Jesus can help them be better people.

Teaching sample

A monologue – Peter is speaking:

It is wonderful being a friend of the Lord Jesus. Andrew (my brother), James and John (our fishing friends), Philip, Nathanael and many more have been Jesus' special friends for about three years. We have seen some amazing things happen. Jesus healed a blind man the other day. The man was sitting by the side of the road, begging for money. When we came near him, the blind man called out, asking Jesus to help him. Jesus asked, 'What do you want me to do for you?' The man said, 'I want to see.' It was great! At that very moment, when Jesus spoke to him, he could see. This happened just outside a town called Jericho.

Today we are walking through Jericho. As always, when Jesus visits a town, there are crowds of people around, wanting to see him and hear him speak. I can see a man hurrying along the road in front of us. I wonder why he is running away from us!

Well! What a sight! The man is now trying to climb a tree at the side of the road! That's a pretty difficult thing to do with the long, flowing clothes we all wear. I wonder why he is climbing into the tree! It seems such a strange thing to do. Perhaps I will be able to see him better when we pass under the tree he has climbed into. Jesus is watching him, too.

Now we have reached the tree, and Jesus is standing still, looking right up into the branches at the man's face. What is going to happen? I can hear Jesus speaking: 'Zacchaeus, come down straight away; I must stay at your house today.'

What do you think?! The man is climbing down from the tree, just as Jesus told him to! Now we can understand why he climbed the tree in the first place – he is so short. I suppose he would never have seen Jesus among this big crowd of people. Did I hear Jesus call him 'Zacchaeus'? Surely this isn't Zacchaeus who collects taxes in this town? I've heard he is a terrible man, and makes people give him much more money than they need to. Then he takes the extra money home for himself. Really dreadful, isn't it? Stealing from people like that. I wonder what made Jesus decide to stay at his house? Well, if I listen, perhaps I'll find out!

We have now reached Zacchaeus' house. A lovely house it is, too. Zacchaeus is a rich man and can afford to live in a big house with lots of nice things. I wonder if he ever thinks about the poor people he has stolen money from, and how difficult life is for them because he has made them poor? I don't expect he ever thinks of them, but only about himself and what he wants.

We are waiting outside the house. Jesus has gone inside to talk with Zacchaeus. Lots of people think it is wrong of Jesus to go to Zacchaeus' home, because they all know what a bad man he is.

Ah! Listen! They are coming out! Zacchaeus looks as though he is going to say something important. He is turning to Jesus. Listen! 'Lord,' he says, 'here and now I give half of all that I have to the poor.'

What?! He's going to give away half of all the lovely things he has bought with the money he has stolen?! Amazing! Listen, he is still talking to Jesus: 'If I have cheated anybody out of anything, I will pay back four times the amount.'

Did I hear that right? Give back four times the amount of what he has taken from people?! That doesn't sound like the old Zacchaeus I've heard about. He must have had a change of heart. Jesus can do that with people. His love for people, even really bad people like Zacchaeus, makes them want to be different.

Now Jesus is talking to Zacchaeus: 'Today salvation has come to this house. For the Son of Man (that's what Jesus calls himself sometimes) came to seek and save what was lost.' Zacchaeus was lost all right! He was more concerned about getting money than pleasing God. But now that he has met Jesus, he is different. He knows now that having lots of money isn't so important after all. Knowing God and pleasing God is much more important. I have noticed that when Jesus speaks to people and they become sorry for their sins, then he seems to give them the power to do good things rather than bad things. I believe Jesus is God's Son whom he promised to send into our world. Only God loves people as Jesus loves people, and only God can forgive our sins.

There are lots of happy people in Jericho today because Zacchaeus has become a follower of Jesus and one of his friends.

A dramatic presentation:

Shalom! Peace! My name is Mary, and I live in a town called Jericho. It is a very pleasant town to live in. There are lots of palm trees growing here, and beautiful rose gardens where the perfume of the flowers is sweet. Our bigger roads are quite busy with people walking through to other towns. Sycamore trees grow along the side of the roads. When it becomes hot in the middle of the day, it is nice to sit under one of these trees and feel cool in its shade. Yes, I like living in Jericho.

It will soon be Passover time for us Jews, which is like a party that lasts all week. We eat special food and go to services in the temple. During the next few days crowds of people will come through our town as they travel to Jerusalem to celebrate the Passover there.

As soon as I have finished my work here at home, I am going out into the street – because I've heard that Jesus is on his way to Jerusalem too, and he will be coming into Jericho today. A few days ago I was told by a neighbour that Jesus had healed a blind man who had been sitting by the road begging. Bartimaeus was the man's name. Of course, I know Bartimaeus and have often seen him sitting by the road myself. It seems amazing that Jesus could just talk to him and take away his blindness and make him see again. Everyone was talking about it. 'Jesus is a very special person,' they said. Well, I missed that, but I am not going to miss Jesus today! Any jobs can wait until later. Why don't you come with me? We could enjoy this outing together.

The streets are busy already. Many of the people are carrying parcels. I guess they are the travellers, the people who are going to Jerusalem for the festival. Oh! A friend of mine from down the road is just coming along. Let's wait for her. Joanna is her name.

Mary:	Joanna! Shalom! Are you going to try to see Jesus too?
Joanna:	Shalom, Mary! Yes, I am! And I feel so excited about it, after all that Elizabeth told me about his healing the blind man the other day. I wonder what wonderful things we will see him do. Mary, who do you think this Jesus is?
Mary:	That's a big question, Joanna. He is someone very special. Perhaps after I have seen and heard him today I will be able to answer that question. Hey, Joanna, look who's hurrying along the road over there!
Joanna:	Zacchaeus! Surely *he* doesn't want to meet Jesus?
Mary:	If Jesus knew anything about Zacchaeus, he wouldn't want to see him. It's not surprising he hasn't many friends. You can't be a chief tax collector and still expect people to like you. Did you hear about the amount of tax money he took from old Zebedee the other day? Zacchaeus is a thief, a cheat!
Joanna:	Look at the beautiful clothes he's wearing today. Bought with money he took from us, I expect! He is in a hurry. Let's follow him and see where he's going.
Mary:	Yes, let's do that – if we can see him in the crowd that's here now. Come on, Joanna! He can move fast, can't he? And it's difficult to see him with all these people around because he's so short.
Joanna:	Where is he now, Mary?
Mary:	I don't know. I can't see him anywhere. Ah well, never mind. Let's keep moving along with the crowd. We don't want to miss Jesus, do we? The people in front of us seem to be slowing down. Look, Joanna! Everyone seems to be looking into that tree. I wonder why.
	The branches are moving! Do you think someone is in it? Listen!
Jesus:	Zacchaeus, come down immediately. I must stay at your house today.
Mary:	Joanna, is that *Jesus*?
Joanna:	Yes, Mary, that *is* Jesus.
Mary:	Jesus is telling Zacchaeus that he wants to stay at his house?

Joanna: Yes, Mary, that's right.

Mary: Well, Jesus can't know what sort of a man Zacchaeus is.

Joanna: Look, Mary! Zacchaeus is doing just as Jesus said. He is coming down out of the tree. I suppose he had climbed the tree because he couldn't see Jesus when he was walking along the road. Poor little Zacchaeus!

Mary: Jesus and Zacchaeus are going along the road towards Zacchaeus' house, so I suppose Jesus was serious about staying with him. Let's follow them, Joanna, and see what happens.

Look, Joanna! Jesus is going into Zacchaeus' house. Perhaps we should wait around for a while. This could be interesting. We may even be able to hear what goes on inside!

(Inside the house.)

Zacchaeus: Look, Lord! Here and now I give half of my possessions to the poor. And if I have cheated anybody out of anything, I will pay back four times the amount.

Jesus: Today salvation has come to this house – for the Son of Man came to seek and to save what was lost.

Application:

Do you remember what Mary and Joanna said about Zacchaeus? He was the chief tax collector. That means that he collected money from the people for the Romans, who were in charge of their country. They said he was a thief and a cheat. And he was. You see, he took more money from people than the Romans said he should, and he kept that extra bit of money for himself. He made other people become poor, but he got richer and richer. Money was very important to him. It bought him nice clothes. It meant he could live in a big house and have servants to do work for him. Do you think he was happy?

(Some members of the group may say 'Yes'!)

Well, deep inside he *wasn't* happy. He had lots of things, but he didn't have many friends and he didn't have peace in his heart. And that was something he wanted. Then Zacchaeus heard about Jesus, and he began to wonder who he was. Some people thought Jesus was the Son of God. Zacchaeus wasn't sure. But he decided that he wanted to see Jesus. That's why he climbed the tree. He couldn't see Jesus while he was standing on the ground because he was so short.

Jesus knew all about Zacchaeus. He knew he was a thief. He also knew that Zacchaeus wanted to be different. That's why Jesus looked into the tree and told Zacchaeus to come down and talk to him. Jesus loved him and wanted to change him.

What was it Zacchaeus said to Jesus? 'Look, Lord! Here and now I give half of my possessions (that means the things I have and my money) to the poor. And if I have cheated anybody out of anything, I will pay back four times the amount.'

Well, that sounds like a different Zacchaeus!!

And what did Jesus say to him? 'Today salvation has come to this house. The Son of Man came to seek and to save what was lost.' Jesus was saying, 'Zacchaeus, you are saved from your old way of life. I came to this world to look for people like you, and to save them.'

You see, as Jesus and Zacchaeus sat in Zacchaeus' house talking, Zacchaeus began to realise who Jesus was. Yes, Jesus is the Son of God, he thought. No one else speaks about God as Jesus does. As he realised this, Zacchaeus knew that he should say sorry to Jesus for all the bad things he had done in the past, and ask for his forgiveness.

We know that Jesus forgave him. 'I came to look for and to save people who are sorry for the bad things they have done,' he said.

Before Zacchaeus met Jesus he was selfish. He wanted to please himself. He didn't care about other people. He didn't care that he made people poor. But when Jesus came into his life, he didn't think about himself. He promised to give back to people much more money than he had taken from them. He was glad to give to others and to help them.

Isn't it wonderful that Jesus can change people that much? I wonder if there are things that you do, or think, or say, which you know do not please Jesus. Well, he can change you. He can change me. I am so glad that he can, and that he wants to.

Try to think of one thing you do which you know is wrong, and ask Jesus to help you to change. His Holy Spirit can do that in you and in me.

Programme for the meeting

This session we offer more help with the teaching rather than the general programme. By now the team will have a good idea what is appropriate for your group. Take a fresh look at previous meetings and see how this one can be improved.

Two new songs that you might like to teach the group are 'Jesus wants me to be like him' and 'We belong to the family of God' (both Causeway Music).

Evaluation

Don't give up on evaluating yourselves just because the programmes have been running for a while. Look back over this session to see how effective your presentation was. If a dramatic approach was used, how well was it applied? How has the programme gone? Have any significant changes or experiments taken place? Don't let yourself fall into a rut!

God's love is very wide

Aim
To show that God's love is so wide that it reaches out both to people who love him and to people who do not.

Objectives
- To show that God wants everyone to know he loves them.
- To show that loving Jesus makes us joyful.
- To show people with learning disabilities that, if God's love is in their hearts, they too can love those who do not love them.

Preparation
YOU WILL NEED
- A map showing Jerusalem.
- Press cuttings of royal visits.

PREPARING YOURSELF
This lesson intends to draw out that God's love is unconditional. The breadth of God's love can cope with rejection.

- Deuteronomy 30:19–20.
- Isaiah 65 (especially vs1–5).
- 2 Peter 3:9.

PREPARING TO TEACH
Read the Gospel accounts of Jesus' entry to Jerusalem (Matt 21:1–11; Mark 11:1–10; Luke 19:28–42; John 12:12–19).

Set the scene for this session's narrative by talking about the Queen's visit to an event, a town, a city or a country, or a foreign dignitary's visit to Britain, which has been televised recently. It may be helpful to use a video recording of the visit, especially if it is not very recent or is to somewhere known to the group. If there has been a royal visit to your area, find and use press reports and photographs of the occasion. Help people to understand the pleasure and happiness experienced on these occasions by those lining the streets to welcome the important visitor. Think of ways to get people talking about royal visits.

Then tell the story of Jesus' triumphant ride into the city, bearing in mind the following points:

- There were greater crowds than usual in Jerusalem because it was Passover time.
- Jesus could tell the disciples what would happen because he is the Son of God.
- Usually a king would ride a stately horse into a city: relate this to what happens at royal visits today, and to peoples' expectations of what a king would be like.
- Note that it was unusual for Jesus to enter a town

in this way, but there was purpose in it. Many in the crowds would witness his arrest and death a week later, and hear of his rising again.
- Make much of the happiness and excitement of the people who welcomed Jesus. Doubtless, Jesus shared in that.
- Draw out the sad side of this event (Luke 19:41–42).

Application:
Emphasise the breadth of God's love: it reaches out to everyone, both to those who shout 'Hosanna!' and to those who were later to call out, 'Crucify him!' Help the group to realise what a wonderful person God is in that he reaches out to all people everywhere. Endeavour to create a sense of wonder and admiration for God and for our Lord Jesus Christ.

Show that God wants *us* to love all the people we know. Because he loves them – each one – he can help us do the same. Make sure the group realises that in refusing Jesus they are turning away from God. And they must understand that there is no other way to find God.

This session is one which may draw out a response. Beware, though, of putting pressure on people or manipulating them. At the same time, they may need help to recognise what they need to do to respond to God's love for them.

Programme for the meeting
Explain that today the talk will be about a special day when King Jesus rode into the big city of Jerusalem, and how the people welcomed him. Encourage the group to sense something of the excitement of meeting King Jesus. Singing some joyful songs will help everyone to feel what it was like to be there.

SONGS
Allow more time for singing this week. Some new songs are suggested below, and the group may need to sing them a few times before they can feel really familiar with them and enjoy them. To give people space and time to get their breath back, allow for periods when the musicians play the tunes on their own while everyone else listens.

- 'We are here together' (CM), a good song to sing as an opener. Makaton signs can be used with it.
- 'God is good – we sing and shout it' (MP 185).
- 'Hosanna, hosanna, hosanna in the highest' (MP 242, sing verse 1 at least twice).
- 'The joy of the Lord will make you strong' (CM).
- 'Make way, make way' (MP 457, this song will need a lot of explanation).

- 'I will enter His gates' (MP 307, this will also need explanation).
- 'Jesus put this song into our hearts' (SOF 299, verses 1 and 4).

TEACHING

After Jesus had been to Zacchaeus' house, he spent time talking to the crowds who followed him. As he came near to a small village close to Jerusalem, Jesus sent two of his disciples on ahead into the village. Now continue with the account of Jesus' triumphant ride, not forgetting to apply it in ways that are relevant to people with learning disabilities.

SHARING

This may be a good time to encourage people to share news of things that have made them glad, especially visitors they may recently have welcomed into their home or into the group.

PRAYER

In response to the teaching, spend time saying 'Thank you' to Jesus for coming into the world because God loves each person. Help people to pray for those they find it hard to love.

Evaluation and review

The teaching session was 'all your own work'! How did it go? Was the language clear and simple? It may still be necessary to write the talk out in full so as to reduce the number of difficult words used.

Was it too abstract? Love is an abstract concept, so we must be careful to talk about it in 'real life' terms. Did the application fit the people it was applied to? Their life experience may be very different and certainly more limited than your own.

Session 8

God wants us to remember his love

Aim

To show that God wants us to remember how much he loves us.

Objectives

- To show that Jesus wants us to remember what he has done for us.
- To help people with learning disabilities to understand and value the communion service.
- To help them be certain of God's love.

Preparation

YOU WILL NEED

- A map showing Jerusalem.
- Bread and preferably a non-alcoholic drink for the wine.
- An article or object that helps you remember a distant friend.

PREPARING YOURSELF

The celebration of 'the Lord's Supper' can become a familiar ritual which has lost some of its impact for us. It would be helpful to read the context in which Jesus celebrated the Passover with his disciples:

- John 13 – 17.
- 1 Corinthians 11:23–32.

PREPARING TO TEACH

This session will consider the most vivid of visual aids. The team should discuss together whether to:

- Explain the communion so that it may be better understood when group members see it take place in church.
- Explain the communion before sharing in it together during the meeting.
- If many of your group are not Christians, explain the communion so that they understand its message.

Terminology varies from 'breaking bread' to 'Eucharist'. Use whichever is most familiar to the group, and stick to it!

Read the Gospel accounts of Jesus celebrating the Passover with his disciples (Matt 26:17–30; Mark 14:12–26; Luke 22:7–20). This special meal took place in the evening of the 14th of Nisan (the first month of the year), on the Day of Unleavened Bread, when the Passover lamb was sacrificed (Luke 22:7; Lev 23:5). Throughout Jerusalem, Jewish families were meeting together to celebrate God's deliverance from Egypt.

Jesus told his friends, 'I have eagerly desired to eat this Passover with you before I suffer' (Luke 22:15). Consider his words and imagine the incredible mix of emotions he must have felt during the meal: the joy of being able to demonstrate that God was making a new covenant with his people; the horror of pending crucifixion and bearing God's wrath against sin.

Those in the group who come from a church background may be familiar with the 'words of institution', but this may simply be recognition of a form of words with little understanding of their meaning. Take care to use the familiar words used in church, as well as simpler terms by which those words can be better understood. For example, the word 'remembrance' is not commonly used these days except in November each year, when we remember those injured and killed in the two world wars.

Keep in mind Paul's warning – 'A man ought to examine himself before he eats of the bread and drinks of the cup' (1 Cor 11:28) – and the attitudes described in Luke 22:24–34. The Lord's supper is for the benefit of sinners, not 'perfect' people.

Programme for the meeting

SONGS

The group will have quite a repertoire of songs by now, and they may want to choose these themselves. There are many songs and hymns about Jesus dying for us. Have the lively songs early in the meeting. Introduce one or two new ones after the talk. Look at these carefully for 'technical' words like 'atonement', 'redemption', 'sacrifice', 'justify' – these are best avoided if possible. New songs include 'Give thanks with a grateful heart' (MP 170) and 'Spirit, Holy Spirit' (CM).

TEACHING

Display the bread and wine on a table, if possible using the plates and goblets from your church.

It would *not* be helpful to go into the significance of the Passover meal for the Jewish people. Simply speak of it as a celebration which took place each year at about the same time as we celebrate Easter. Check that people understand the word 'celebrate' (link it to birthday or Christmas celebrations). It was an important family time for Jewish people, when they ate special food and talked about the good things God had done for them. It was a time to say 'Thank you' to God. Jesus and his special friends celebrated the Passover together. Retell the account in Luke 22 (vs7–20 only), setting the scene for this meal and bringing out its new significance. Make the following points clearly:

- Jesus was not saying that his body was made of bread and wine! If this is your first attempt to explain symbols, prepare your explanation carefully. Don't try to be too deep.
- When Jesus said, 'Take the bread and eat it. This is my body which is broken for you', he knew what appalling events would take place later that day, culminating in his death.
- Similarly, in the wine he was anticipating the blood he would shed to provide a basis for forgiveness. Make sure people understand that there was wine in the cup when he said, 'This is my blood.'
- Jesus wants us to remember what he did for us on the cross – until he comes back for us. A memento of a friend and how it reminds you of them could illustrate how the Lord's supper reminds us of Jesus and what he has done for us.
- The point of this remembrance, in the context of this series, is that it shows us how much God loves us.

REFLECTION AND PRAYER

If you are going to take the Lord's supper together, this would be an appropriate time to do so. Explain what people have to do, how much bread to take, and so on.

If not, spend time in prayer encouraging people to tell Jesus they are grateful for his death for them. Endeavour to help them understand God's individual love for them.

Jesus and his disciples sang a hymn at the end of their time together: you may wish to do the same. Verses 1 and 2 of 'Thank You Jesus' (MP 633) would be ideal.

Evaluation and review

A demanding and important issue was dealt with at this meeting. It may produce a desire in some to begin taking communion. Let church leaders know beforehand what you will be covering in this session – you may need to discuss all the implications with them. Encourage the team to help group members who attend the same church as themselves to recall the significance of the Lord's supper next time it is celebrated.

God's love is real

Aim

To show that God's love is very real and strong.

Objectives

- To show that God not only says he loves us, but demonstrates the greatness of his love.
- To show people with learning disabilities that they are loved by God.
- To help people with learning disabilities respond to God's great love.

Preparation

YOU WILL NEED

- A map showing the city of Jerusalem, the Garden of Gethsemane and the place where Jesus was crucified.

PREPARING YOURSELF

This is the most familiar and important lesson so far in this series. The most important preparation is yourself! Spend time reading and reflecting on the accounts of Jesus' arrest, trial and death.

- Read the Bible verses listed below, and 1 John 4:10.

PREPARING TO TEACH

Each of the Gospel writers gives a detailed account of what happened to Jesus during the hours leading up to his death – more detail than can be included in this teaching session. Omit Peter's denial and keep strictly to the arrest, trial and death of Jesus. These events can be found in:

- Matthew 26:36–68; 27:1–53.
- Mark 14:32–65; 15:1–39.
- Luke 22:39–53,63–71; 23:1–49.
- John 18:1–14,19–40; 19:1–42.

With a rather long narrative to encompass, it would be helpful to bear in mind one important aspect in each section of this study:

The arrest

Emphasise that Jesus was in control of this situation. He was not taken by surprise when the soldiers, led by Judas, came to arrest him. He took the initiative at that time and literally floored them.

The trial

Jesus' trial was long and grossly humiliating. In fact, it consisted of two trials: the first was ecclesiastical, and the second civil. Each contained three stages. In the first, there was a preliminary hearing before Annas (John 18:12–14); then trial by the Sanhedrin (Matt 26:57); and another hearing later, just after daybreak (Matt 27:1). The civil trial involved a hearing by Pilate, Herod and then back to Pilate. The important issue to bring out is the fact that Jesus was not found guilty of any wrongdoing, in spite of devious attempts to ensure that a verdict of guilty was passed on him.

Jesus' death

The fact Jesus was condemned to die on a cross was not simply the result of people's angry desires: it had been planned in heaven as the supreme expression of God's love for the world he had created. We should not cover up the wicked actions of the Jewish leaders, or the shameful and humiliating way in which Jesus was dealt with; but the overriding theme for this session should be Jesus' death as the full demonstration of God's love. Such love requires a response. Make this clear without manipulating your hearers.

Both the story and the concepts it requires for understanding are familiar to us. Will they be familiar to those with learning disabilities? For example, they may know the word 'trial' but do they know what it means? Similar words include 'arrest', 'court', 'judge', 'condemn', 'guilty', 'innocent', 'crucifixion', 'execution', 'death sentence', 'crown of thorns'. Those who watch the television news may understand some of the terms, but generally the language is outside their life experience. Think carefully how you can make yourself understood, or the aim of the lesson will not be achieved.

In view of the importance of this, we have provided part of the teaching session to illustrate how the account can be retold to focus on the main issues and avoid words which are not likely to be understood.

The personal application requires careful preparation. Don't attempt it piecemeal, but have it as the climax and conclusion of this session and of the whole series. Endeavour to:

- Bring out the theme of God's great love for us.
- Show that God loves each person, and that was why Jesus died for each of us.
- Show that Jesus died for our sins: he had none of his own for which to be punished.
- Encourage the group to make a response, eg being sorry for wrong things done, having trust in Jesus. Explain carefully how they might do this, what words they might use.

There is a lot to say in this session. Have a short break between each of the three sections, to give time for a suitable song or for the musical instrumentalists to play.

It may be desirable for your group to extend this theme over two or three meetings rather than cram everything into one and achieve little or nothing. Be guided in this by the extent to which your group members have received the teaching so far.

Teaching sample

Last time we were together we talked about the special meal Jesus had with his disciples. When he gave them the bread to eat he said, 'This is my body, which is broken for you.' And when he gave them wine to drink he said, 'This is my blood poured out for many.' He was sharing with his special friends a simple meal which he used to show them that very soon he was going to die. Today we are going to think about Jesus dying on the cross for us.

The arrest:

After the meal, Jesus and his friends sang a song of praise to God. Then they walked to a quiet place just outside Jerusalem, a garden where there were lots of trees. Jesus liked to go to this place to get away from all the crowds in the big city. It was a good place to go to when he wanted to pray. And he wanted to talk to his Father now.

Jesus went a little way in front of his disciples, and knelt down to pray to God his Father in heaven. Jesus knew that in a few hours he was going to die on the cross. He asked God to help him. The Bible tells us that God sent an angel from heaven to help Jesus.

Jesus went on praying, and he was very upset because he knew he was going to suffer awful pain in his body and hurt in his heart. Then he got up and went back to the disciples, and found them asleep. It was evening time and getting dark, and they were very tired. Jesus woke them and asked them to get up and pray.

Jesus and his friends saw lights shining through the trees. Then they heard people talking quietly. There was a group of people coming through the garden, straight towards them. As well as carrying lights, like torches, to see where they were going, some of them were carrying swords, and some of them were holding sticks. Judas, who used to be one of Jesus' friends, was showing these people where Jesus was. Jesus knew why they had come. He is God's Son, and he knew all that was going to happen to him.

This group of people must have looked and sounded quite frightening. Jesus' disciples were very scared. Jesus asked the men with torches who they were looking for. They answered, 'Jesus of Nazareth.'

'I am he', said Jesus. 'I am the one you are looking for. Let my friends go free. I am the one you want to arrest, to catch and hold on to.'

Jesus turned and said to his friends, 'I could ask my Father God to help me by sending thousands of angels to rescue me. But I must die, because that is what my Father and I have planned.'

(Break.)

The trial:

The men who arrested Jesus had been sent by the Jewish leaders who hated him. The leaders were all waiting in the High Priest's palace for the soldiers to bring Jesus to them. For many weeks the Jewish leaders had wanted to kill Jesus.

They were jealous of him because a lot of people believed he was the Son of God. They didn't want people to follow Jesus. They thought that the only way to stop this happening was to kill Jesus. To make this seem like a good thing to do, they had Jesus arrested and brought into their court.

In our country, if a person is arrested because he has done something bad, like robbing or killing someone, he has to go to court. The court is the place where people try to find out whether the person really has done something bad. If he has, then they decide how he should be punished.

Jesus was taken first to the Jewish court and then to the Roman court. The people in charge of the courts were not fair. The Bible tells us the Jewish leaders wanted to find something bad that Jesus had said or done, so that he could be punished and they could get rid of him. But they could not find anything. So they got people to tell lies about him. Then the High Priest asked Jesus a very important question: 'Are you the Christ, the Son of God?'

'Yes, it is as you say,' Jesus replied.

The High Priest turned to the others in the court and said, 'You heard what Jesus said – he is the Son of God! If anyone says he is God's Son, he should be put to death! What do you think?'

'He should die,' they said.

Jesus is the Son of God, and he was right to answer the High Priest. But the High Priest and the other men in the court did not really believe that he is God's Son. They did not want other people to believe in him either. They were so rude to Jesus: they spat in his face and hit him with their hands. Then he was tied up and handed over to soldiers so that he could not get away. The soldiers took Jesus to Pilate, the Roman governor. Pilate was in charge of the area where they lived, and Jesus had to go to his court.

The Jewish leaders told Pilate that Jesus had done a lot of wrong things. Pilate asked Jesus questions. He decided that Jesus had not done anything wrong, and he wanted to let him go free. Pilate said to the people, 'I have questioned him in front of you all, and there is no reason for him to die. He has done nothing wrong.' But the people shouted back, 'Crucify him! Kill him on a cross!' In the end Pilate gave in to them and let the soldiers have Jesus. The Roman soldiers dressed Jesus up in a long red coat, and they put a crown made from twigs with thorns on his head. Then they pretended he was a king and got down on their knees in front of him. They spat at him and hit him with a stick. That is not the way to behave in front of a king! Then they took him away from the court. The Jewish leaders had got their way. Jesus was to be killed by being nailed to a cross made of wood, even though Pilate said he had done nothing wrong!

(Break.)

The death:

The soldiers forced a man to carry the heavy wooden cross and take it, behind them and Jesus, to a place just outside Jerusalem. This place was called Calvary. There they nailed Jesus' hands and feet to the cross and stuck it firmly into the ground. That must have hurt Jesus' body such a lot. But I think his heart was hurt more by the cruel words of the Jewish leaders. They called out to him, 'He saved other people but he cannot save himself! If he really is the Son of God, let God rescue him now!' Jesus was the Son of God, and God could have helped him. But God sent Jesus into our world to die in our place for the bad things we have done. Other people also shouted rude and cruel things to Jesus as he was dying in great pain on that cross.

Jesus prayed to his Father again. 'Father, forgive them,' he said, 'for they do not know what they are doing.' It is hard to understand just how strong and real Jesus' love is. He asked his Father to forgive the people who are being so horrible to him. Isn't that amazing?

Some of Jesus' friends and his mother followed him all the way out of Jerusalem to Calvary. They watched as Jesus hung upon the cross. I'm sure they wished they could help him, but there was nothing they could do. Jesus saw his mother standing near his special friend, John. He loved his mother and wanted to help her. He knew how awful she was feeling, having to watch him suffer so much. Jesus said to John, 'Take my mother and look after her.' Wasn't it wonderful that in all his pain he showed such love and care for her?

Then something strange happened. It was 12 o'clock, mid-day, lunch-time – which is usually the brightest time of day – but it became very dark for three hours. It seemed as if it was suddenly night-time. Jesus called out from the cross, 'My God, my God, why have you left me?' Jesus knew why God his Father was not near to him at that moment, but he felt so awful and so lonely that he had to cry out like that. He was lonely because God his Father was punishing him, Jesus, for all the sins in the world. It is hard to understand just how awful this was for Jesus.

Then Jesus died.

At that moment a terrible earthquake came. The ground shook and big rocks were split in two. A Roman soldier, who had stood and watched Jesus die on the cross, saw the earthquake. He said, 'Surely he was the Son of God!' The soldier realised that God had made the sudden darkness come. God had made the earth shake and the rocks split, because his dear Son Jesus had died on that awful cross. The soldier felt terrible. He had helped to kill the Son of God!

Later that day Jesus' body was taken down from the cross, wrapped in cloth and laid in a cave in the rock. A big stone was placed at the front of the cave, so that no one could touch Jesus' body or take it away.

(Prepare an application which shows how Jesus' death is important for each person at the meeting.)

Programme

The programme should reflect the seriousness and sense of wonder at Jesus' death for us. Create an opportunity for the group to make their personal response. The team should be prepared to help individuals in this. A time of prayer together prior to the meeting would be desirable.

After the teaching, encourage quiet reflection on what has been said. Team members could try to help people talk about what they think of Jesus dying for them.

SONGS

A good song to sing before the teaching session is 'Jesus died at Calvary' (an echo song). Other songs include 'I worship you, O Lamb of God' (explain first that 'Lamb of God' is a way the Bible talks about Jesus) and, as a response song, 'Jesus, take away all my sin' (all these from Causeway Music).

Look back with hope

That's it! You may be wondering why at first you were so worried about getting involved. But you have started something you cannot easily stop. For the sake of the people you have met in the sessions, I encourage you to continue. Now you can do so with far greater confidence than you had a few weeks ago!

The way in which the sessions in this book have been put together is intended to teach *you* as well as those you have been teaching. You will have noticed a variety of methods for approaching subjects and presenting truth. You should now be able to continue preparing programmes, drawing on your own resources. Should you feel that this is not practical, for whatever reason,

you will be relieved to know that Causeway PROSPECTS has a series of teaching packs which follow through on what we have covered here, so that you can continue to build up a more complete view of what God is like to the people with learning disabilities coming to your group.

As you look back, you will probably see weaknesses and failings, but make sure that you also see blessings and benefits. Reflect on what you have learnt along the way, not least about yourself, from the people with learning disabilities with whom you have shared these sessions.

Resources

Organisations

Causeway PROSPECTS
P O Box 351, Reading RG1 7AL; tel (0118) 950 8781, fax (0118) 939 1683, e-mail causeway@prospects.org.uk PROSPECTS is a Christian voluntary organisation which values and supports people with learning disabilities so that they can live their lives to the full. It operates as two divisions:

- Living PROSPECTS supports about 130 people with learning disabilities in residential and day services in England, Wales and Northern Ireland.

- Causeway PROSPECTS exists to inform and encourage Christians in outreach and ministry to people with learning disabilities. It supplies teaching and other materials. Over 100 local groups are associated with Causeway PROSPECTS throughout the British Isles.

BUild, the Baptist Union initiative with people with learning disabilities
Secretary: Rev Siôr Coleman, 12 Barford Crescent, Kings Norton, Birmingham B38 0BH; tel (0121) 433 5417. BUild is a network of families and individuals concerned to encourage greater awareness of people with learning disabilities in the churches and denomination. It has published a limited range of materials to encourage and assist the integration of people with learning disabilities into church life.

The Shaftesbury Society
16 Kingston Road, London SW19 1JZ; tel (0181) 239 5555. A Christian organisation providing residential services to people who are elderly or who have physical or learning disabilities.

Walsingham Community Homes
1331–1337 High Road, Whetstone, London N20 9HR; tel (0181) 343 5600. An ecumenical Christian organisation providing residential services to people with learning disabilities in the UK.

MENCAP
123 Golden Lane, London EC1Y 0RT; tel (0171) 454 0454. The principle campaigning organisation for people with learning disabilities and their families. It has a network of local parents' groups, clubs and activities for people with learning disabilities. It also runs a large number of residential services for people with learning disabilities throughout the UK.

Down's Syndrome Association
155 Mitcham Road, Tooting, London SW17 9PG; tel (0181) 682 4001. An organisation providing support and information for families and for individuals with Downs' syndrome. It has a network of local groups throughout the UK.

National Autistic Society
393 City Road, London EC1V 1NE; tel (0171) 833 2299. Supports families, and individuals with autism, through regional groups.

ARC (The Association of Residential Care)
ARC House, Marsden Street, Chesterfield S40 1JY; tel (01246) 555043. The primary association of organisations providing residential services for people with learning disabilities, including both large charities and small one-off ventures.

Supplies
Causeway PROSPECTS publishes and supplies a large range of materials for use in worship and ministry to people with learning disabilities. A full list with prices is obtainable from the Reading office.

SONGS AND MUSIC

Causeway music tapes
The Father himself loves you I and *God's love is great II*
A total of 40 songs and music specially written for use with people with learning disabilities.

Causeway music songbook
Music and words of the songs on tapes I and II.

Causeway songbook
Words only of 70 recommended songs for Causeway PROSPECTS groups, printed on coloured paper to simplify their use by people with learning disabilities.

- *Copyright law:* Free use may be made of songs for which you have bought the songbook or the professionally made acetates. Making up acetates or songsheets will require a license from Christian Copyright Licensing Ltd, 26 Gildredge Road, Eastbourne, E Sussex BN21 4SA. If your church has a license, this should cover the Causeway PROSPECTS group meetings. A CCL license is not needed for songs from Causeway Music.

TEACHING MATERIALS

'God is...' series
Supplements which continue the theme of this book are available. Titles include 'God is Holy', 'God is forgiving', 'God is powerful' and 'God is faithful'.

'Who is Jesus?'
An extensive series on the person and work of Christ.

Tape teaching packs
The ministry to people with learning disabilities at Spring Harvest in recent years.

The Easy to Read version of the Bible
A translation from America ideally suited to being read to and with people with learning disabilities, and for use by those who are able to read for themselves. Available in the UK only from Causeway PROSPECTS.

TRAINING
* Information on regular regional workshops is available from the Causeway PROSPECTS office.
* A modular training manual will be available from 1998.

SPECIAL OFFER
Beautiful ... or What?! is an album written by Phil Thomson and Adrian Snell. It provides a moving insight into learning disability, public and professional attitudes, and the impact on family life. There is a series of musical 'snapshots' of a young woman with learning disability, seen in relationship with her rag doll, which reveals God's perspective on her life. Available, while stocks last, from Causeway PROSPECTS at the special price of only £9 for the CD or £6 for the cassette (+ postage & packing). Contact the Reading office.

What is God like?
GOD IS LOVE

CAUSEWAY
prospects

Group News-Sheet

Jesus shows us what God is like

Philip said to Jesus, 'Show us the Father.'

Jesus said to Philip, 'Anyone who has seen me has seen the Father' (John 14:8–9).

Today we are asking a very big question: 'What is God like?'

Does anybody know?

Yes! The Bible tells us about God, and Jesus shows us what God is like.

That's good. We can all see what God is like – he is like Jesus.

When Jesus was here in our world as a man, he called some people to follow him and to stay with him as his special friends. We call them his disciples. Jesus talked to them about God, his Father. One of the men that Jesus called to follow him was named Philip.

The night before Jesus died on the cross, he told his disciples that he was going back to heaven and in heaven he was going to get ready a special home for them. They could not understand what he was saying. Philip said to Jesus, 'Lord, show us the Father and that will be enough for us.' Jesus said to Philip, 'Anyone who has seen me has seen the Father.'

Jesus was saying to his disciples, 'I am God. You know me, because you have spent time with me. Anyone who knows me knows what God is like.'

We cannot see Jesus now as Philip did. But we can learn about Jesus in the Bible, so we can find out what God is like.

You can read about this in the Bible, in **John chapter 14, verses 8 and 9**.

God's love is kind

Jesus was kind to Jairus and his wife, and to their daughter.

'Give her something to eat,' he said (Mark 5:43).

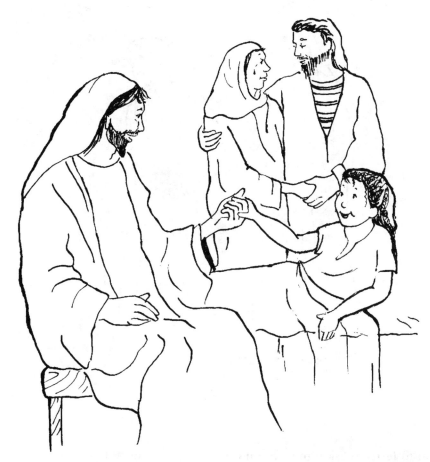

Jairus and his family lived in a town called Capernaum. They were a happy family – until Jairus' twelve-year-old daughter became very ill.

Jairus and his wife were very worried about their daughter. They had heard about Jesus, and when he came near to their town Jairus thought he would ask Jesus to help.

'My daughter is dying,' he told Jesus. 'Please come and put your hands on her, so that she will get better.'

'I will come with you and see your daughter,' Jesus said.

A friend of Jairus found him and said to Jairus, 'Your daughter is dead. Don't bother Jesus any more.' Jesus heard this and told Jairus not be afraid but to trust him.

In Jairus' house, Jesus went to the girl who was lying still. She was dead, as Jairus' friend had said. Jesus took hold of her hand and said, 'Little girl, get up!' She opened her eyes and got up. Jesus said to her mother, 'Give her something to eat.'

Jesus is kind to people because he loves them. He is kind to us because he loves us. He shows us that God cares about us all the time and gives us what we need.

Jesus is such a lovely person to know.

You can read about this in the Bible, in **Mark chapter 5, verses 21 to 43**.

God's love is strong

Jesus loved the young man, and he loves us too.

'Jesus looked at him and loved him' (Mark 10:21).

A young man ran to Jesus to ask him a very important question: 'What must I do to enjoy life with God now and when I die?' Jesus told the man what God's rules were. The man knew all about them, and said he had always tried to keep God's rules.

Jesus knew that the man really had done this, but he could also see that the man was not keeping the biggest of God's rules. This was to love God with everything we have, to love God best.

'There is one thing wrong with you,' Jesus said. 'If you want to enjoy life near to God, you must go and sell everything you have and give your money to help poor people. After that, you can enjoy life with God here and in heaven. Then come and follow me.'

The young man was very rich, and he loved his money and all the lovely things he had bought with it. When Jesus told him to give them away, he felt very sad. He didn't want to give them away. He loved them more than he loved God. He walked away from Jesus. He could not do what Jesus asked him to do.

Jesus was sad that the man loved his money more than he loved God. As he watched the man walk away, he felt strong love in his heart for him.

Jesus loves everyone, even the people who do not love him. We find it hard to love some people. What do we love best? We need to think about that.

You can read about this in the Bible, in **Mark chapter 10, verses 17 to 22.**

God's love is great (big)

Jesus shows us that God cares for a lot of people.

Jesus felt sorry for the big crowd which had come to see him (Mark 6:34).

A big crowd of people followed Jesus around the countryside. They wanted to hear what he was saying about God, and see him do special things. Jesus loved everyone in that big crowd, and talked to them for a long time about his Father, God.

Jesus' special friends could tell that the people were getting hungry, and they wanted to send them home. Jesus knew they needed food straightaway.

The disciples brought five loaves and two fish to Jesus. He told them to ask the people to sit down on the hillside. He thanked his Father for the food and gave it to the disciples to give out to the people. There was enough for everybody to eat and feel really full up!

Jesus did not want anyone to go home weak and hungry. He fed them all. Because he is God's Son he can do anything, even make a little food big enough to feed an enormous crowd.

Jesus didn't just love a few people in the crowd – he loved them all and wanted to help them all. He wanted to show them that God's love is very great, very big. He knows it is important that we feel loved. God gives us friends and family to love us and care about us. He gave us Jesus, who came and lived in our world and showed us what God is like.

God is love and his love is great! He loves and cares for a lot of people.

Jesus wants us to work with him to show people that God loves them too. Ask him to help you to do this.

You can read about this in the Bible, in **Mark chapter 6, verses 30 to 44.**

God's love is a caring love

Jesus really cared about the blind man and listened to him.

'What do you want me to do for you?' Jesus asked him (Mark 10:51).

Jesus and his special friends were leaving Jericho, and a crowd of people were following them. A poor blind man was sitting by the side of the road, asking people to give him a little money so he could buy some food. He could not work to get money.

When he heard that Jesus was coming along his road, he began to shout out: 'Jesus! Son of David! Have mercy on me!' The people told him to stop shouting, but he did not. In fact he shouted even louder. Jesus heard him calling out and asked some people to bring the man to him.

'What do you want me to do for you?' Jesus asked the blind man. 'I want to see,' he said. Jesus spoke to him again, and the man could see! First he saw Jesus, and then he saw the crowds of people all around them. Then he looked up and saw trees and birds. Jesus had healed him and now he could see. It was wonderful! He followed Jesus along the road, shouting his praises to God.

Jesus cared about the blind man. He wanted him to know that he had heard him call out for help. He wanted him to know and to feel God's love for him.

God says we are important to him, too. He listens to us when we talk to him. He cares about us and will help us, too.

You can read about this in the Bible, in **Mark chapter 10, verses 46 to 52**.

God's love changes people

Jesus loves people who are not very nice to know, and his love changes them.

Jesus came 'to seek and to save what was lost' (Luke 19:10).

In the city called Jericho there lived a very lonely man whose name was Zacchaeus. He was lonely because he was a thief. He collected tax money from the people and asked them for more than they needed to give him. The extra money he took home for himself.

One day Zacchaeus heard that Jesus was coming through Jericho. He had heard people talking about Jesus, and he wanted to see him. A lot of people wanted to see Jesus, and there were crowds out on the street. Zacchaeus was rather short and could not see above the taller people around him. He noticed a tree and made up his mind to climb it so that he could see when Jesus came that way.

Jesus knew that Zacchaeus was in the tree, and he knew that Zacchaeus wanted to meet him. When Jesus came to the tree, he stood still and looked up into it. Zacchaeus was so surprised when Jesus spoke to him. 'Zacchaeus, come down straight away,' he said. ' I must stay at your house today.' Zacchaeus climbed down quickly and was very happy to take Jesus to his home.

Zacchaeus knew that Jesus loved him just as he was. And he wasn't a very nice person. He found out now who Jesus was, the Son of God. Because Jesus loved him, Zacchaeus began to feel sorry for all the bad things he had done. 'Lord,' he said, 'I am going to give half of all that I have to the poor.'

Jesus' love had touched his heart. Now Zacchaeus wanted to live for God. He showed that he really was sorry about the bad things he had done by giving back to people more money than he had taken from them. That was amazing!

You can read this in the Bible, in **Luke chapter 19, verses 1 to 10.**

God's love is very wide

Jesus loved all the people.

'Blessed is the king who comes in the name of the Lord.'

'As he approached Jerusalem and saw the city, he wept over it' (Luke 19:38, 41).

Jesus usually walked quietly into the towns and villages he visited. But his visit to the big city of Jerusalem was going to be different. He was going to ride into Jerusalem on the back of a donkey.

Many of the people who saw Jesus coming took branches from the trees and waved them in the air. They took off their coats and laid them down on the road for Jesus to ride over. They shouted out together, 'Blessed is the king who comes in the name of the Lord!' They were very excited! Jesus had done some wonderful things, and they wanted to praise God for these. Jesus felt happy as he sat on the back of the donkey and heard the people praising his Father, God. He knew his Father was pleased too.

Jesus rode on along the road which went right into the big city of Jerusalem. There were angry people there who wanted Jesus to stop the people from praising his Father. There were big crowds of people who did not believe Jesus was God's Son. Jesus felt sad when he saw them. He felt so sad inside that he cried. He had come to show people what God is like, but many of them did not believe him.

Jesus' heart was full of love. He loved the people who were excited and who sang praises to God. He loved the angry people and those who did not believe in him. God's love is so wide, it stretches across the world to everyone. No one is left out. He wants us all to know that he loves us, whether we love him or not.

When we know that someone loves us, we want to love them too. God sent Jesus so that you can be sure he loves you. Do you love him?

You can read this in the Bible, in **Luke chapter 19, verses 28 to 42**.

God wants us to remember his love

Jesus wants us to think about him.

'Do this in memory of me' (Luke 22:19).

Jesus said to his two friends, Peter and John, 'Go and get a special meal ready for us, so that we can celebrate together.' He told them just where to go and what to do. Peter and John enjoyed doing that for Jesus.

Later, Jesus and his other special friends came to the house where Peter and John were ready and waiting for them. They sat down to eat together.

Jesus had some very special things to say to his friends. He held up a cup and said, 'This is my blood poured out for many for the forgiveness of sins.' There was wine in the cup, not blood. Jesus was thinking about what was going to happen to him later that day, when he died on a wooden cross. He was thinking about the blood that would come from his sore hands and feet, and head and side. But he knew that God, his Father, could forgive people their sins because he died like this.

Jesus picked up some bread. 'Take the bread and eat it,' he said. 'This is my body given for you.' Jesus knew that even before men nailed his body to the cross, they would hit him and beat him. His body was going to look broken. But he let this happen for us, for our good.

Jesus said to his friends, 'I want you to eat bread and drink wine together, as we have done today, to remember me and my painful death for you.'

Christians everywhere do this together to remember Jesus and what he has done by dying on the cross. Jesus wants us to remember him and his love for us, which goes on and on.

You can read about this in the Bible, in **Luke chapter 22, verses 7 to 23**.

God's love is real

God says he loves us, and he shows us that he loves us.

'The Son of God who loved me and gave himself for me' (Galatians 2:20).

Jesus went with some of his special friends to a quiet garden near Jerusalem. He wanted to pray to his Father, God. Jesus knew that in a few hours he was going to die on the cross. He asked God to help him. God sent an angel from heaven to help Jesus be strong.

Some men came to find Jesus and caught hold of him. They took him to the High Priest's palace and made him stand in front of the people. Some of them wanted to get rid of Jesus, and they told lies about him. Jesus had done nothing wrong.

The High Priest asked Jesus an important question: 'Are you the Christ, the Son of God.'

'Yes, it is as you say,' Jesus replied.

The High Priest and the other men in the palace would not believe that Jesus is God's Son. 'He should die because he says he is God's Son,' they said.

Then the soldiers there were cruel and rude to Jesus. They spat in his face and hit him with their hands. They took him to the Roman governor, who was called Pilate. Pilate thought Jesus had not done anything wrong. He wanted to let Jesus go free. But the people shouted at him, 'Crucify Jesus! Kill him on a cross!'

Pilate became frightened of them, so he let the soldiers take Jesus to a place near Jerusalem, called Calvary. They nailed Jesus' hands and feet to the cross, and fixed the cross into the ground. This hurt Jesus' body a lot. But his heart was hurt more by the cruel words of the Jewish leaders, who called out to him, 'He saved other people, but he cannot save himself.' Jesus could have saved himself, but he chose not to because he wanted to save us from our sins.

Jesus prayed to his Father again. 'Father, forgive them,' he said, 'for they do not know what they are doing.' Jesus' love is so real that he can forgive even people who hate him.

You read what happened in the Bible, in **Luke chapters 22 and 23**.